Old-Time
Preacher Men

compiled by Mary H. Wallace

Old-Time Preacher Men

compiled by Mary H. Wallace

©1992 Word Aflame Press
Hazelwood, MO 63402
Reprint History: 1998, 2001

Cover design by Tim Agnew

All Scripture quotations in this book are from the King James Version of the Bible unless otherwise identified.

Printed in the United States of America

Printed by

WORD AFLAME®PRESS
8855 DUNN ROAD
HAZELWOOD, MO 63042-2299

Library of Congress Cataloging-in-Publication Data

Old-time preacher men / compiled by Mary H. Wallace.
     p. cm.
    ISBN 1-56722-000-2
    1. United Pentecostal Church International—Clergy—Biography.
2. Pentecostal churches—Clergy—Biography.   I. Wallace, Mary H.
BX8780.Z8A423 1992
289.9'4'0922—dc20
[B]   92-11302
                                        CIP

Contents

1

MACK DIXON ABBOTT

by Marvin E. Abbott

Born on March 31, 1894, my dad, Mack Dixon Abbott was one of ten children of a Baptist minister who was also a farmer. Dad had four uncles, a sister (whom he won to the truth), and one brother who were ministers. When he was a child, Dad's parents moved to western Oklahoma and lived in the area of Elk City and Sayre.

In 1915 he married Esther Joseph and they continued to farm. Within a few years Marvin E., Earl V., Chester L. and twins, Oleta and Vinita were born to the Mack Abbotts.

In 1930 Dad and his family visited an Assembly of God church. During the service, tongues and interpretation went forth: "God is calling, God is calling." Tall, slim, six-foot-four Mack Abbott stood up slowly and went to the altar. He said, "There was a light from above surrounding me that led me to the altar." Mother followed him and eventually all five children came to God.

Later the family heard of a little Pentecostal church across the tracks. One evening we went and heard Brother Jim Barber preach baptism in Jesus' name, the

Holy Ghost, speaking in tongues, and the oneness of the Godhead. Dad sat by the kerosene lamp studying his Bible for hours trying to prove that preacher wrong. "I've heard my dad preach the trinity doctrine all my life. That surely has to be right."

The more he studied the more he realized that Brother Barber was right. He and Mother accepted the message and were baptized in Jesus' name with the children following suit not long after. Soon Mother received the Holy Ghost and seven months later Dad received the Holy Ghost in a private home in Elk City, Oklahoma, at 4:00 A.M.

A year later, Brother Barber took another church, and for over two years, Dad helped keep the church together. In about 1932 C. P. Kilgore held an open-air revival in Elk City, and a close friendship developed between Brother Kilgore and Mack Abbott, continuing until Brother Kilgore's death. Brother Kilgore preached a couple of revivals for my father in Roswell, New Mexico. Shortly after the last one, my dad helped conduct Brother Kilgore's funeral.

In 1934 after they fasted and prayed, God called Dad and Mother into the full-time ministry. They went to Sayre, Oklahoma, then on to Vernon, Texas, where we lived in a tent and held an open-air revival with over a hundred converts. His old pastor, Brother Jim Barber, came and took over.

After a year, Dad left the work with Brother Barber and evangelized several months in West Texas and Oklahoma. Then his sister asked him to come to Roswell, New Mexico. There the Lord helped him build a church that is still standing. He preached on the courthouse lawn and held open-air revivals in the park, where I, his eldest son, came to God. After renting a building for a while, he built an adobe church in 1938. Within a few years, God called his three sons, Marvin, Earl, and Chester, into the ministry, along with his two sons-in-law, Boyd Cates and Charley Cooper.

Dad was in Roswell for over thirty years, and most of his ministry was like a revival. Hundreds came to God. A few months before his death, Dad told me thirty-six active ministers had gone out from that church in Roswell. Some of them are Tommy Hudson, pastor in Mesa, Arizona, district home missions director, and leader of the Indian work; B. H. Havens, pastor in Farmington, New Mexico; John Wright, who started the church in Brownfield, Texas; and Cletus Floyd, who started the church in San Luis Obispo, California. As of this writing, Dad has three grandsons in the ministry: Ronald Abbott, pastor in Tulare, California; David Abbott, pastor in Scottsdale, Arizona; and Ricky Cooper, assistant pastor in Warsaw, Indiana.

Dad served as a presbyter with the Pentecostal Church, Incorporated, before the merger of the United Pentecostal Church. After the merger he was elected the first district superintendent of the Texico district, which included New Mexico, West Texas, and Colorado at that time. He served as superintendent for eight years. During this time Sister Eastridge was in the church in Roswell for about two years. Dad helped her get the Indian work started in New Mexico, where her son, Jerry, still carries on the work.

Dad was a great debater and debated many Church of Christ ministers and some trinitarian Pentecostals, winning some people through these debates. After his father had preached over fifty years in the Baptist church, Dad finally convinced his father of the truth of Jesus Name baptism.

Mack Abbott was known as one of the best preachers on the Godhead and the name of Jesus. Forty years old before he began his full-time ministry, Dad really put himself into the work and always said, "I'm gonna preach until I die." And that he did, until the Lord called him home on March 8, 1967. My dad was one of the greatest preachers I have ever known.

Mack Abbott

The Mack Abbott family

Calvin Samuel Albert and Laura Webb on their wedding day, June 30, 1935.

2

CALVIN SAMUEL ALBERT

by C. S. Albert

On January 15, 1913, at Reber Place in St. Louis, Missouri, John David and Margaret Ellen Post Albert welcomed my birth. Ethel, Lela, Ruth, and Roy made our family. They attended the Christian Church.

When I was eight Aunt Sarah, enthused with the Holy Ghost, visited us. Father opposed her message, but after studying Acts my mother wanted the Holy Ghost. Aunt Sarah took me and her to a mission on Cardinal Street pastored by B. H. Hite. Mother received the Holy Ghost, speaking in other tongues. Benches served as pews and the services were not programmed, but the glory of God filled this humble place. Later Brother Hite rented a long, narrow building on Easton Avenue.

One day I felt conviction and found Mother cleaning the bathroom, so I told her how I felt. "Kneel here beside the bathtub," she said. I confessed my sins and in February 1921 Brother Hite baptized me in the name of Jesus.

Our family met two great ladies, Mother Mary Barnes and Mother Moise (Maria Christina Gill Moise), who operated a rescue home for girls and a mission located at 3333 Washington. Then my sister Lela received the Holy Ghost.

After several years, Brother Hite moved the mission to 1414 North Grand Avenue, an upstairs hall seating two hundred. On October 15, 1925, my pastor said, "Don't you feel you are old enough to receive the Holy Ghost?" That night the Holy Spirit fell on hundreds, including me and my sister Ruth.

Then Pastor Hite felt led to build a new church. We moved into a new building located at 3105 Cass Avenue in 1926. We called it Gospel Tabernacle, a place of miracles. After being healed, people went home leaving crutches and canes, which hung on the wall as a silent testimony.

One night a little girl led a blind man up for prayer. Brother Hite prayed, then asked the man if he could see. The man said, "No." Brother Hite prayed again, putting his hands on the man's eyes. Nothing happened. Brother Hite asked again if he could see. The man answered, "I can see light and people far away." Brother Hite prayed once more, "Let the man have full vision." The man began to shout, "I can see!" We had revivals and healing services every night but Monday.

God called me to the ministry at fifteen. My mother advised me to study the Word, fast, and pray. Pastor Hite appointed me as youth leader and song leader. At eighteen, he put me on the church board "to see how the church functions."

In May 1934 I met Laura Webb, who had been attending church regularly and was devoted to the Lord. On June 30, 1935, we were married in the church by Brother Hite.

In the middle of the Depression the mortgage on the church came due. The loan company notified Brother Hite that we must have thirteen hundred dollars soon. When he read the notice to the church, total silence prevailed. After weeping and praying Brother Hite asked, "Does anyone have anything to give?" No one did. "We have prayed for God to provide. If God gives me any money, I'll give it. How many will do the same?" A few responded. "God will help us."

At that time he was an official with the Pentecostal Church, Incorporated, with headquarters in Dallas, Texas. A man asked him to come to Texas. When he arrived, the man offered him one thousand dollars if he would move to Dallas to work for the P.C.I. "I cannot accept, because God told me not to leave St. Louis," Brother Hite said. The man gave the check to him anyway saying, "Do what you want with it."

When Brother Hite returned, he said, "This check is mine. The man gave it to me but I'm going to give it as I pledged." Then he raised the other three hundred dollars. Before the due date, the church debt was paid.

In 1931 I attended my first Pentecostal Ministerial Alliance convention at Gospel Tabernacle. In 1932 the convention in Little Rock elected Brother Hite as leader. The ministers voted to include local churches so they changed the name from Pentecostal Ministerial Alliance to Pentecostal Church, Incorporated.

About 1928 a tall, blond man came to Gospel Tabernacle. Evangelical in faith, Harry Branding hungered for God. He liked what he felt so he came back. He received the Holy Ghost, was baptized in Jesus' name, attended church, accepted responsibility under Brother Hite, and began preaching. A pastor had left a mission church at Eleventh and Hickory, so the people called Brother Branding to help. When they needed larger quarters he purchased a Methodist church building at Thirteenth and Gravois, remodeling it into a spacious church.

In 1939 the Pentecostal churches of St. Louis, East St. Louis, Granite City, and Belleville organized youth groups and asked me to lead monthly rallies. I also suggested a giant Labor Day youth rally. This rally ran for a while, then Missouri made it a district function. The last several years they held the rally at Westphalia. Then they divided it, holding one at the campground and the other in southeast Missouri. The rallies lasted over forty years.

Feeling God leading him, Brother Hite had first come to St. Louis in 1920 with only $3.50. As he was walking down a street, he met a beggar who asked for help. "I only have $3.50 but I'll give you half of it," Brother Hite promised. When folks asked for money for food, he always gave. If an unknown preacher needed services, he invited him to preach and gave him an offering.

He encouraged young men in the ministry. At his suggestion I applied for local license with the P.C.I. on April 1, 1942.

By this time my family had increased. Dorcas Ruth was born July 31, 1936, and on July 8, 1941, Calvin Samuel, Jr. arrived. At age three Dorcas contacted whooping cough. Brother Hite prayed for her and God healed her instantly.

Revival continued at Gospel Tabernacle with power-packed services. George and Helen White came, repented, and received the Holy Ghost. Brother White felt a call to go to Java and asked his wife, Helen, "Where's

Java? Let's go to the library to find out." Helen told her husband, "God called you to Java. He didn't call me." After prayer, she also heard the call. The Whites prepared themselves, then traveled to the churches, sharing their burden and raising financial aid.

In 1943 Superintendent Howard A. Goss ordained me at the P.C.I. conference in Hot Springs, Arkansas. At this time the constituents voted to move the P.C.I. headquarters from Houston, Texas, to St. Louis.

The Pentecostal Assemblies of Jesus Christ was another Oneness organization whose chairman was W. T. Witherspoon and whose headquarters was in Columbus, Ohio. Both organizations embraced practically the same doctrine.

In 1944 when the P.A. of J.C. held its convention in St. Louis, Harry Branding of the P.C.I. and Oliver Fauss of the P.A. of J.C. met to draft a resolution to merge. In 1945, the two groups accepted the resolution. They chose the name of United Pentecostal Church and elected Howard A. Goss as general superintendent, W. T. Witherspoon as assistant general superintendent, and S. W. Chambers as general secretary.

I worked with Brother Hite and at my job at Central Pattern Company. He asked if I felt led to full-time ministry. There were no Bible colleges for men to attend, but we counted forty-eight preachers who had gone out from Brother Hite's church. He told me of a church in Little Rock, Arkansas. "Why don't you and your family take this church?" My wife and I prayed. Finally I just walked off the job and came home. "We've got to find the mind of God," I declared. We prayed and then the next morning prayed again.

While we prayed, the telephone rang. Sister Oscar Smith from Roadhouse, Illinois, said, "I'm trying to open a church in Roadhouse and we need a pastor." We moved there and pastored for six months. Since Sister Smith had leadership ability, there seemed no need for us to stay longer.

Detroit, Michigan, needed pattern makers so we went there. After a few miserable months, we realized that this was not God's will. "We must move back to St. Louis," we decided, so we packed. Then Pastor Johnson from the church on Schoolcraft knocked on our door. "Brother Branding from St. Louis wants you to call." I went to a pay phone and called. "Hannibal needs a pastor, Brother Albert."

"We wouldn't be interested, Brother Branding." I explained "We're moving back to St. Louis tomorrow."

"Well, stop by the church and let's talk about it," Brother Branding insisted. "Every time I pray about a pastor for Hannibal, Calvin Albert has stood before me."

So we visited the storefront where Frank and Faye Osbourn were ministering in Hannibal. The building was for sale, so we purchased it. Six rooms upstairs made our home. We moved to Hannibal on July 1, 1945.

At first we had seventeen in Sunday school, mostly women and children with little financial support. I got a job in Quincy, Illinois, and paid most of the church bills. We drove ninety miles to St. Louis for fellowship.

One afternoon in 1946 Brother Alexander Raby preached a fellowship meeting in Hannibal. Conviction seized several who prayed in the prayer room. As we prayed the power of God fell. Slain by the Spirit, seekers lay on the floor. Prayer lasted through the service, then more people crowded in. Six received the Holy Ghost.

Robert Dougherty came for three nights of services. "Get a half-page ad," he advised. The ad cost fifty dollars! About thirty attended, and our building seated seventy-five. "Plenty of room," we said. The first night every seat was full, so we asked him to stay. "Only if you'll get a larger place." The town officials said, "Use the armory building; it seats three hundred." We advertised on the radio and the armory filled. We received $150 in the offering!

Several received the Holy Ghost. Many were healed and we baptized our first candidate, Laura Majors, in the Mississippi River. Later we baptized several others in Bear Creek, including Bill Inlow, who got up from a sick bed, and Sister Embree. She had not planned baptism but waded out in her dress clothes eager to obey God. A widow woman, she had four married children plus three small boys when she came.

In simple faith, she practiced our teaching. She told of an urgent need. "I told the Lord, 'You promised to supply all our needs and Pastor said that we could stand on the Word of God.'" So she laid her Bible on the floor and stepped on it, telling the Lord, "I'm standing on the Word." Later I told the saints to claim by faith what they needed. "If you need a new suit or a new dress, go to the store, select it and trust God."

Sister Embree walked through the business area by Lucke's Maytag washer store. The owner, Mr. Lucke, asked, "May I help you." She said, "The Lord is going to give me this washer." Mr. Lucke looked at her, amazed. She told him about the sermon. "I need a good washer. I support my three little boys doing laundry for folks."

"When do you want it delivered?" Mr. Lucke asked.

"Oh, I can't take it now. I don't have the down payment."

"When do you want it? I'll deliver it first thing Monday and you can pay as you collect from your washings."

That night Sister Embree laughed and cried at the same time as she testified about her miracle.

George White, Jr., son of the missionaries to Java, preached one of our first revivals, and then Claude Young came. When Brother Young preached an eight-week revival for L. D. Segraves in Kennett, Missouri, some country music singers received the Holy Ghost. They had so many invitations they had no time for worldly appearances.

They came to Hannibal, and as they sang, the power of God swept over us. Sinners ran to the altar. Some of the musicians were Chuck Grey, Carl and Ola Denny with their band, and Norman and Maxine Luna. They returned for years.

In 1949 Claude Young preached again. One morning he said, "I dreamed I preached high in the air over Hannibal!" Later he asked, "Why don't you use the radio? What an opportunity to get the truth to Hannibal!" In 1950, I asked about radio costs. "Forty-two dollars a half-hour." I asked folks to pray about a broadcast. Sister Laura Majors waved a dollar saying, "I want to give the first dollar." Others gave. We started broadcasting the next Sunday when Brother Young began our revival. After service, he exclaimed, "Brother Albert, this is the fulfillment of the dream I had about preaching high over Hannibal."

The Lord helped us acquire the Congregational Church building that had stood empty for a year on Eleventh and Broadway. We had looked for a larger building but felt it was futile. One day a real estate man asked, "Would you be interested in selling your church? I have a man who wants it."

"Yes, if we could get the right price," I replied.

"How much do you want for it?"

"We've never considered a price."

"Meet and set a price and I'll be back," he said.

We paid 5,000 dollars for the property, so we decided on 8,000. "Let's ask 8,500 to give me a commission for selling it," the agent said.

Not expecting him to agree so readily, I said, "Just a minute, we can't sell until we have somewhere to go."

"There's a church building at Eleventh and Broadway for 25,000 dollars," he mentioned.

"No way! We don't have that kind of money," I answered.

He kept coming back. "I'm trying to get it for you."

"Mr. Brice, you know how much money we have. We'll have 5,000 dollars left after we pay our loan of 3,000 dollars on this building," I said firmly.

"Just make an offer on the building," he insisted.

"I can't make an offer," I tried to explain. Mr. Brice went back to the sellers and told them that 12,500 dollars was all we could afford. They let us have that building right on the main artery to downtown Hannibal for 12,500 dollars. God answered our prayers! We moved the last of October 1948.

Built at the turn of the century, the church needed a new roof, a new furnace, and a paint job. After we finished, it was a very impressive building with carved trim and stained glass. A beautiful place to worship!

When we began broadcasting over station KHMO in 1950, many people came. We raised the money first, then I felt free to preach if the broadcast was paid for. One night just before we went on the air, we still needed twenty-six dollars. No one responded. A drunk man came to the platform and paid the entire bill. Many of the people who came said, "I went to this kind of church when I was a kid." We broadcasted each week from May 1950 until the fall of 1983.

I worked all those years and also pastured the church. But in July 1959 I quit my job to give full time to the church.

We had an evangelist who prayed for the sick and God blessed. Word spread and the sick came for prayer, including a jeweler from Decatur, Illinois. When the minister called for a prayer line, I saw two men help the jeweler down the aisle. He could not walk. He had short legs from having rickets as a baby. After prayer, he walked down the aisle alone.

In regular church services, we often asked the church to fast and pray on Tuesday and then come on Thursday night expecting a miracle. One young mother, Frances Keller, brought her month-old baby for prayer. Later she returned rejoicing. "My baby had not been using her left arm. After prayer, the baby began moving the arm. When I got to the doctor, I told him about it. 'Yes, I know.' he told me. 'I didn't tell you that the nerve in that arm was dead, leaving the arm useless. But the Man upstairs has done His work.'"

Dorothy Keller, one of our older saints, stepped off a curb and broke her hip. She was reading her Bible when the doctor came to see her. The doctor told us, "She'll have to go to a nursing home. Due to her age and the place where the hip is broken, healing will take a long time." After a few days in the hospital, Sister Keller felt that God had touched her. "I want to go to church. If I can just get to church and be prayed for, I'll be all right." When the doctor came in, she told him, "I want to go home."

After examining her, the doctor said, "That little black book you've been reading has helped you. You can go home on crutches, but you'll have to be careful."

That night Sister Keller came, and when we prayed, she shouted and danced right off her crutches. I was scared, but she walked out with her husband carrying the crutches. In her eighties she was still walking.

One Sunday night Carl Nelson told me, "I've been witnessing to a man whose wife is dying with cancer. I've invited them to church for prayer. His wife is in a wheelchair and can't sit up long. I told him we'd help and that we'd bring pillows so she could lie down on a pew."

When Brother Carl saw the couple, he and the men helped bring her in. After the preaching during altar service, several saints gathered to pray. After a while she sat up. The saints kept on praying until she began to walk around the church. Her anxious husband and some of the saints followed her. She came back and sat down. Their little three-year-old girl looked bewildered, so she lifted the child up on her lap. Her husband wept, "My wife has not been able to do that for three months!" Later they came back to the church without the wheelchair. She even went down to the river on fishing trips with her husband.

Our thirteen-year-old Dorcas complained about pain in her wrists. My worried wife called the doctor. When I arrived home, the doctor was there. "We need to get this girl to the hospital within the next ten or fifteen minutes," he said, then called the hospital for a bed. "I'll meet you there in about ten minutes."

After he left, I prayed, "Lord, we've always preached healing and now our daughter is sick. We need you, Lord."

My wife got Dorcas ready. As we left she cried, "Don't take me to the hospital. I'm healed." She felt the Lord touch her as she went out the door, but we weren't sure. "Let's go ahead," I said. "The doctor will be expecting us." When we got there, they examined her and said that she had rheumatic fever. My wife made plans to stay that night.

"You should go home because she'll probably be here six months to a year," the nurse said. After the nurses and doctor left, Dorcas said, "The Lord healed me as we went out the door. I want to go home." She kept saying she was all right, so the doctor gave us permission to take her home. "But she'll have to be kept very quiet."

We went home, but she went to church that night, played her accordion, and sang in a trio. I thought, *Well, if she drops dead here, this is what she wants. There's nothing I can do.*

Healing is such a miracle that it's hard to comprehend. Dorcas married at eighteen and still has good health.

Through the years I served in different capacities in the Missouri District of the U.P.C.I. When Brother B. H. Hite passed away in 1948, he was the superintendent of Missouri District. Brother Branding was secretary. He was elected as superintendent, and I was appointed as district secretary and served until 1952. I served as presbyter of our section from 1945 to 1984, when poor health forced me to retire from the church I established in 1945 and pastored for over thirty-nine years.

When I retired, we had a good group of ministers. Through the years we had grown to eight churches in our section: Hannibal, Mexico, two churches in Moberly, Macon, Canton, Montgomery City, and Kirksville. I also served as editor of *The Voice of Missouri District*, our district paper, as well as secretary of the Sunday school department of Missouri, and later as Sunday school director. For a time I served on the board of Gateway College of Evangelism in St. Louis. Later I taught a class on Corinthians. I feel that my life has been enriched by all these tasks.

God gave me another desire of my heart when He allowed me to make a trip around the world. We left Missouri the first of February 1973 and returned in March. Our friends the George Whites, missionaries in Java in Indonesia for many years, had invited us to come to Java. For Christmas of 1972, the church had given us a trip to the Holy Land, so we decided to combine this trip with the visit to Java. On this trip we ministered in England, India, Thailand, Indonesia, the Philippines, Japan, and Hawaii. It was a memorable, once-in-a-lifetime trip.

In January 1974 we ministered in Mexico City, Mexico. In May 1980 Brother Glen Smith, superintendent of the Caribbean, invited me to Puerto Rico to preach their pastors' conference and speak to the Bible school students. Afterwards we flew to Port-au-Prince, Haiti, where Brother Vannoy took us to two of the Haitian churches.

In May 1982 we hosted the annual Missouri District

spring conference at our church in Hannibal. The district planned a surprise banquet in my honor. The guests included Mayor John Lyng of Hannibal, Congressman Harold Volkmer, a number of leading Hannibal businessmen, General Superintendent Nathaniel and Jean Urshan, Missouri District Superintendent Guy and Lillie Roam, Illinois District Superintendent M. J. Wolff and his wife, Stanley Chambers and his wife, many other fellow ministers, and the saints from Hannibal. As my son led me around to read the posters that honored me for sixty years in Pentecost, I was overwhelmed.

In May 1985 the Missouri District planned a ceremony renewing our wedding vows in celebration of our golden wedding anniversary. Our children planned another surprise celebration in honor of our golden wedding anniversary on June 28, 1985, in Illinois.

The Lord was so good to allow us to build a wonderful body of precious saints in Hannibal, Missouri, over a period of nearly forty years. In September of 1983, my strength began to abate, yet I tried to keep on with my activities as pastor. By November I was completely helpless. I had to give up the church and the office of sectional presbyter that I had held since 1945.

Our daughter, Dorcas Willis, took us to her house in Chicago so that her family could take care of me. The doctor said, "Parkinson's disease, arthritis, and congestive heart failure." Then in December I took the flu. Brother Chambers, Missouri District superintendent, and Brother Manning, district secretary, flew to Chicago to see about me. They asked the Missouri churches to pray especially for me and, praise the Lord, He answered prayer. At this writing, four years later, my health has been renewed, and I have traveled and preached in a number of churches throughout Missouri and Tennessee.

Besides our two children, Dorcas and Calvin Jr., we have nine grandchildren and fourteen great-grandchildren. I am looking forward to attending the great jubilee some day in the New Jerusalem.

Editor's Note: Desiring to return to their native state, the Alberts moved to Bridgeton, Missouri, and attended New Life Center, pastored by their old friend, Guy Roam, and his son, Jim Roam. Calvin S. Albert died on September 18, 1990.

First Pentecostal Church, 1100 Broadway, Hannibal. Missouri.

The Alberts 30th wedding anniversary; Calvin S. Albert Sr., Calvin Jr., Dorcas Ruth Albert Willis, Mrs. Calvin S. Albert, Sr.

3

JOHN H. DEARING

by Joyce MacBeth Morehouse

In the early 1900s, a young cowboy from Idaho heard about a revival in a nearby Baptist church, so he and his buddies decided to go and see what was taking place. His mother, praying that God would save her son, went along also.

At the end of the message, the evangelist gave the appeal and the Lord spoke to the cowboy's heart. "John, go give your mother a kiss, then go to the altar." And John did just that.

Born November 7, 1880, John Dearing had never become a church member. Following his repentance he joined the church where he had found the Lord. Here he first heard the Jesus Name message. A lady from Maine who was holding special services made the statement: "There is a Cornelius here and God has sent me to you with a message." Then she told about Jesus Name baptism and the Holy Ghost with the evidence of speaking in tongues.

Years later this "Cornelius" sat teaching at the Newcastle Bridge convention in New Brunswick. With his ever-present asthmatic spray in his hand, he taught in the open air in a grove, as he preferred to do due to his severe struggle with asthma. He captivated his listeners with the story of his "Cornelius" experience.

"I went back on the job the next day. That night I crawled under the wagon, where I had been sleeping on the ground, but not to sleep, for the stars were saying, 'Glory to God! Hallelujah!' Next morning I got up, put on my yellow pants, a khaki shirt, and my straw hat, then tucked my Bible under my arm and headed for the hills of Kentucky."

This "Cornelius" became an outstanding leader in early Pentecost. A powerful Bible teacher, he left behind a legacy of tracts and Bible lessons still used throughout our ranks.

Brother Dearing felt led of God to spread the good news, and one of the brethren from Maine asked him to come and evangelize. There he joined a group of workers who were evangelizing in Charleston. Later they moved to a hall on Water Street in Bangor. After a while the others drifted into various fields of labor, leaving Brother Dearing with the Bangor work. He remained in the general area from 1920 to 1940, but the effects of his efforts were more far-reaching than Bangor, for his ministry touched numerous ministers and communities. New Brunswick was among the major recipients of the glorious message he preached.

During one of his early visits to New Brunswick, Brother Dearing met his future wife, Anna Miller from Debec, near Woodstock. Brother Edgar L. Grant pastored in Woodstock at the time, and Brother Dearing baptized him in Jesus' name along with Brothers Leonard Parent,

Milford, Wynn, and Quincy Stairs, and several others.

After Brother Dearing had pastored Bangor for a few months, word got around that he had a "new doctrine," and many wanted to hear what he had to say. In November 1920, he accepted an invitation from Brother Grant to speak to the Woodstock convention, a ten-day session of teaching and fellowship among the Pentecostal pioneers of New Brunswick and Maine. Several had already received the Holy Ghost, one of the first being Hubert Perkins, who received this experience in Fielding in 1912. Others who assembled were Sisters C. C. Clark, Kitty and Noreen McLellan, Brothers Billy Ellis, Charlie and Harvey Flewelling, F. Harold Bickford, William Killam, and Moody Wright. Brother Earl Jacques, who had only been converted a few months, was in the group, as were Brothers Ralph McCloskey, Leonard Parent, and Milford and Quincy Stairs.

Brother Dearing ably expounded his biblical insight on the Jesus Name doctrine, but as he sat quietly on the platform beside Brother Grant, it was difficult to realize this humble man would have anything astounding to say. Little did the convention body realize that in a short time Brother Grant would be called home and their convention speaker would serve as his replacement in a leadership capacity.

During the next year, 1921, at the age of forty-six, Brother Grant became seriously ill and Brother Dearing sat at his bedside during the illness, notebook in hand. He took notes as Brother Grant selected three songs to be sung at his funeral, then preached his own funeral sermon from II Timothy 4:7. At the funeral Brother Dearing preached from this text, and the congregation sang the three hymns.

After the passing of Brother Grant, Brother Dearing led the young flock of Jesus Name Pentecostals in Maine and New Brunswick until 1926, when Brother Jacques took over. He did an excellent job, encouraging the work of God by letters and visits. The youthful pastors especially appreciated his wisdom.

Brother Harvey Howe wrote of his counsel: "I was about twenty when I met Brother Dearing and his wife in Bangor, Maine, in 1930. This man was a wonderful blessing in my life. Let me mention a few of the things that he taught me a minister should or should not do. . . ." And he went on to relate some incidents. He told how Brother Dearing, on hearing he was keeping company with a young lady, took him aside and urged him to seek God's direction for his life as a wife could either prove to be a blessing or a hindrance to his ministry.

Between 1920 and 1940, Brother Dearing traveled and evangelized. He also taught a while at Brother Rohn's Northwest Bible Training School in Caldwell, Idaho. During one such venture, he and his wife were making the four-thousand-mile trip back east from Lewiston, Idaho, with only $30.25 in their pockets. The fare to Star, Idaho, was $31.86. When their money had taken them as far as they could go, the conductor put them off. They spent the night in the depot. Next morning, Anna changed shoes, and there, in the toe of her other shoes, was a five-dollar bill, so they boarded the next train and went on. Brother Dearing also told of the empty flour barrel. He and Anna put their heads in the empty barrel and sang praises to God.

John and Anna Dearing had two sons, Clement and

David. One incident stands out to Clement as having made a great impression on his childish mind. In the early days of Pentecost, they moved about pitching their tent wherever they felt directed of God. A group of rowdies would throw rocks at the tent each night. One night as they were throwing stones, the ringleader was in the wrong place at the wrong time and had his eye put out with one of his own gang's rocks.

In 1933, a group of New Brunswick brethren attended the Pea Cove convention in Maine, where Brother Dearing was the camp speaker. In the group were Brothers Stanley McConaghy, Clement Hyde, Wynn Stairs, and Earl Jacques. The speaker walked across the platform weeping as he said, "Look at these young men. I am so proud of them!" And well he could be, for he had a great part in their training. Brother McConaghy later stated, "Of all the men that ever sacrificed for this Jesus Name truth, John Dearing was the greatest."

It was not always easy to proclaim the truth. When he first came to New Brunswick, some of the brethren were skeptical. One night Fred Keirstead had a strange dream. He thought he had piled his wood up neatly, with great care, and someone came by and pushed it over. He felt sure Brother Dearing was responsible for knocking down his well-documented and orderly doctrine.

Brother Dearing believed in God's law and order, and he always looked for the logic in any situation. He often said that God works His wonders, but He is logical.

During Brother Dearing's lifetime, his heart was gradually weakened by bouts of asthma, but he patiently endured this until, in the year of 1940, a doctor from Howland, Maine, felt that he might be able to treat him successfully. He went to Howland, where he stayed with Brother Howe's in-laws. Brother Howe mentioned that he sometimes studied Bible lessons at Brother Dearing's bedside when the latter was too sick to get up.

When the doctor had given him just three days to live, Brother Howe went to visit him. Brother Howe later said he would never forget the extreme swelling and the deteriorating state of Brother Dearing's physical body, but likewise his anticipation as he spoke of going to be with his Lord. On December 9, 1940, John Dearing slipped away to his eternal home.

While at Brother Rohn's Bible school, Brother Dearing helped prepare a course of study called the *Pentecostal Home Study Course.* It has since become well-known in our ranks in preparing individuals for the ministry. The lessons cover over one hundred subjects and several complete books of the New Testament.

The sacrifice he made for the truth was not in vain, for today there are numerous godly men and women, saints and preachers alike, who love the truth of the message he was willing to bring to a hungry people. How his heart will rejoice when we join him around God's throne!

John Dearing and his wife, Anna, leave Lewiston, Idaho
going east with only $30.25 in their pockets and faith in
God in their hearts.

4

CHARLES CLIFFORD DECKARD

by Audrey E. Deckard

"Then Peter said, Silver and gold have I none; but such as I have give I thee: In the name of Jesus Christ of Nazareth rise up and walk" (Acts 3:6).

"Can a maid forget her ornaments, or a bride her attire? yet my people have forgotten me days without number" (Jeremiah 2:32).

These two texts represent sermons that span forty-five years in the ministry of Charles Clifford Deckard, better known as C. C. Deckard.

On June 5, 1931, my mother and I attended a Holy Ghost revival in a small storefront building pastored by Lena Spillman. The presence of the Lord in songs and testimonies filled the place as Sister Spillman introduced "our young fiery evangelist."

As he approached the podium, I suddenly knew he was for me. I whispered to my mother, "That's the one I want for my husband."

"Quiet! He's probably already married," she said.

"I know he is for me and the Lord has kept him till now."

Without further comment from me but after a proper introduction and a short courtship, we were married on June 28, 1931. After a church service we were called to the front, and as the pianist played softly the old hymn "Rock of Ages," the minister pronounced us man and wife.

Clifford Deckard was born April 30, 1910, in a small community called Handy, south of Bloomington. He was the second of four children (one died in infancy). As a young child he learned what heartaches were. His father passed away when he was six years old. One year later his mother followed her husband in death. Clifford's next years were spent with whomever would take him. Eventually he was put in an orphanage. At fifteen he ran away and began to learn the ways of the world.

Somehow the Lord kept his hand upon this orphan boy. One incident shows how God watched over Clifford. When he was eight he was offered a part in a school play, provided he would bring fifty cents for the material needed for the costume. He hurried home to tell about his part in the play. When he told his story, the lady of the house replied, "We feed and clothe you out of the goodness of our heart. You don't need to be in the play. It's all foolishness!" A heartbroken boy trudged back to school for the afternoon, sobbing his heart out. As he neared the school, suddenly he spied a shiny fifty-cent piece in the gutter. "Now I can be in the play!" he shouted. Was there Someone who did care for him?

Leaving the orphanage, Clifford roamed the country, sleeping and eating where he could, working at odd jobs. Between jobs he often rode the freight trains. As the wheels turned they seemed to chant a refrain, "You're going to hell, you're going to hell. . . ." He pondered the message as he rode.

In February 1929, he was in Indianapolis, Indiana, where he engaged in light- and middleweight fighting contests and frequented poolrooms. On his way to the boxing ring one night, he passed a theater with a large sign out front: "THE KING IS COMING!" Thinking it was a movie, he went in. What a surprise awaited him!

As he listened to the Word of God, it lodged in his heart. As he stood longing to go forward, a voice spoke, "If you go, others will follow." He was the first to be baptized and filled with the Holy Ghost, with sixty-six others following in a few weeks.

Sister Spillman took him into her home, treating him as a son. At last he had a home with those who cared. He lived with the Spillmans until we married. He was the first preacher saved under her ministry; a great number saved since then are serving the Lord throughout the world.

After the campaign, he went to his aunt's home in Terre Haute. She had given away her possessions as she was not expected to live but a few weeks. After hearing Clifford's testimony about God's healing power, his aunt returned to Christian Tabernacle. After prayer she was healed and lived many years to hear her nephew preach the gospel.

While he was hitchhiking along the highway, a voice said to him three times, "Quench not the Spirit. I have called you to preach." A little further on he saw a Bible in the grass, dirty and soiled. The voice spoke again, "Proclaim my Word. It is trampled under the foot of man."

Afterward, he put forth great effort to reach the lost. With a bucket of red barn paint and a brush, he printed

"OBEY ACTS 2:38" on every corner sidewalk for blocks around the church. When his old buddies saw him coming, they called out, "Here comes the Holy Ghost! Six months from now he'll be back with us." But God had planted a desire in his heart that they knew nothing about. His Bible was always with him. When asked why he marked it, he replied, "I'm marking up my Bible to beat the devil."

We evangelized in southern and western Indiana. Our first daughter, Martha Sunshine, was born January 6, 1933. That year in February my husband was invited to Madison, Indiana, for a revival. The baby and I stayed home, so he asked Victor Jordan to drive with him in our roadster with the rumble seat. God blessed, and souls were saved. People were baptized in the Ohio River after the ice was broken. They rejoiced for two blocks back to the church in wet clothes. No one caught pneumonia either!

Scant food failed to fill empty stomachs in this revival, but one dear saint brought rock candy and jelly for snacks. They ate jelly and bread then rock candy. Offerings were as scarce as meals.

After two weeks Brother Deckard announced, "Monday morning we are going home."

After the service the pastor asked, "How? Only seventy-five cents in the offering!"

"The Lord will provide," my husband answered firmly.

The next morning at 8:30 a young couple knocked at the door and asked if they could ride to Indianapolis. "We'll buy the gas," they offered. With snow on the ground and winter winds blowing around their heads, they rode that rumble seat some 120 miles. Feeling that

God had blessed them, the two young preachers divided the seventy-five cents.

Revival fires flamed. Sacrifices mattered little as long as God led. Brush arbors, schoolhouses, storefronts, living rooms, and the open air provided pulpits. We carried food in the trunk of the car and our clothes on a pole across the back seat. We cooked by the road and often slept in the car.

We had eggs, tomatoes, and oranges thrown at the car and food stolen out of the trunk, but when evening came and hungry souls streamed down the road and over the hills to church, we rejoiced. At one revival we came out after church to find our car stolen! A few weeks later God provided another car. He never fails! At one baptismal service in the river under a bridge, bystanders spat on Brother Deckard and the baptismal candidates. He only said, "Jesus was spat upon and I'm no better than He."

On November 7, 1934, God blessed us with a son, Paul Eugene. At church on Christmas night we heard that one of our closest sisters in the church had died, leaving a husband and two small girls. Going home, my husband said, "I must feel what Carl feels to sympathize with him. That's how I prayed tonight." The next morning he learned how Brother Carl felt. Our darling seven-week-old baby had been called home during the night. Sister Spillman had Sister Nolaz's funeral in the morning, our son's that afternoon.

We had built a small house. We were faithful to our home church and preached on weekends. Several churches had asked my husband to pastor, but he did not feel led to do so at that time. We learned to hang paper, which gave him time to take meetings. The company he purchased supplies from said, "You hang paper until you save $100 to $150, then go and preach it up!" In this way we could go when others could not during the Depression.

Our second child, Esther Pauline, was born January 9, 1935, and our third, Elsie Louise, on January 28, 1937.

During World War II my husband worked in a defense plant. Soon he was offered a promising position over a three-state area. Already hampered, he knew this job would limit his church work even more, so he refused the offer. Shortly thereafter his foreman remarked, "Cliff, you are a very valuable man to our company, but you must decide between your job and your church activities."

Without hesitation Clifford replied, "I don't have to decide. That decision was made some years ago." Removing his shop apron and picking up his tool chest, he quietly walked out. Since then we were able to say with David, "I've never seen the righteous forsaken nor his seed begging bread."

We pastored three churches in Indiana until 1949 and evangelized as far as Florida. One New Year's Eve he preached a rally in Buchanan, Michigan. Representatives from the Benton Harbor church approached him about becoming their pastor. We prayed and two weeks later went there for a service. After Sunday school we were invited to a saint's home for dinner. It was a humble home, with no refrigerator, and only a two-burner coal oil stove; however, the meal was delicious. During the conversation my husband said, "Sister Bryant, I'd love to see you have a good electric refrigerator and stove." With tears in her eyes she said, "Brother Deckard, I don't need those, but we do need a pastor." That settled it. He took over the pastorate of the Benton Harbor church.

In November our second son, Charles David, was born.

Here is an article my husband wrote in December 1958, detailing the trials and victories in pursuit of the work.

"The Apostolic Tabernacle on the corner of Seeley and McGuigan in Benton Harbor is a lighthouse for the Jesus Name message in this town. It has not always been so, for trials and tests have threatened to tear down the truth we stand for, but by the grace of God and faith in Him who died for us, we are still on the same corner, still teaching and preaching the only gospel.

"During the Christmas season of 1948 I preached for a group of people that had no pastor. On January 28, 1949, I took over the pastorate. They had a small basement church, built too low in the ground. At each rain much water had to be swept out before we could have church.

"We could not find living quarters, so we drove 187 miles from Indianapolis every weekend. On June 10 we rented a house fifteen miles out in the country. We lived there until September, then returned to Indianapolis. Another winter we drove to keep the church together. The following winter we rented the house next to the church.

"On June 12, we saw our last service in the basement, and services were held in our house for the next two months. We completely tore down the building, raised the floor thirty-two inches, enlarged the basement, and started to build. We moved back in the building on August 11.

"The following summer we continued with a building 30 feet by 77 feet with Sunday school rooms, a kitchen, and a dining hall in the basement. The pastor's office and nursery are on the first floor. We have also installed an organ and upholstered seats.

"The first few months were hard, with eight saints and fifteen to twenty in Sunday school, but now our Sunday school has an average of 115. Our church is now practically debt free. The Lord has been gracious to us.

"We have three married daughters, all filled with the Holy Ghost as children and serving God. We have only Chucky at home and are still thanking God that we do have him. At the age of five weeks, he was given one chance in a thousand to live, but God healed him. In December of 1954, the doctors gave him up with sleeping sickness and paralysis of the lower limbs. He lost all of his senses but hearing. We brought him home on December 24 in a semi-coma. Scarcely had he been in the house one hour until he tried to climb out of his bed and spoke for the first time in thirteen days. Those few words sparked faith in our hearts, and although he spoke no more for a few days, we believed God could and would heal him. Chuck has come a long way in these four years and is doing well in his schoolwork. When we took Chucky back to the specialist in February, the doctor called his nurse and said, 'Would you come here? I want you to see a miracle.'"

In 1964 we turned the pastorate of the church over to Brother James O'Haver and went to South Haven, Michigan, where we pioneered another work. Brother Crider is now pastor of that church. Our son, Charles David, had a heart attack and passed away on December 13, 1966. He was seventeen-years-old, a sophomore in high school. Only a few days before he had told a visiting minister, "I have only one desire, to live for the Lord."

Upon the death of our son we moved back to Indianapolis and our home church. While helping build a new edifice there, Brother Deckard stepped on a nail. Because of his diabetic condition, the injury did not heal. Consequently he lost his leg in 1971 and the second leg in 1972.

Prior to losing his legs, he was asked to pastor the church in Niles, Michigan. He decided to accept only if the vote was unanimous. It was unanimous! After losing his first leg, he desired to give up the church, but one of the dear saints told him, "If President Roosevelt can run a country from a wheelchair, I'm sure God can give you strength to pastor us." He preached on artificial legs and climbed ladders to remodel the church, outside and in, with the help of faithful saints. Through all of his hospitalizations, God gave us a wonderful assistant pastor, Brother William Mitchell.

In the spring of 1975, my husband resigned, and we purchased a motor home and evangelized through Indiana and Arkansas, then to Florida. Usually one or two of the grandchildren were with us.

In December of 1975 we went to our daughter's in Des Moines, Iowa, where he preached his last sermon for Brother Wayne Butcher. There he suffered his third heart attack. After his being hospitalized there for a time, we came home, where in January of 1976 he suffered a stroke and passed on to his reward. At the last Michigan monthly rally before his death, held in Three Oaks, Michigan, Brother Deckard rejoiced and danced before the Lord to the amazement of those present.

He served on the Michigan District Board from 1950 until his illness caused him to resign. From the first campground at Little Fish Lake in 1960 until 1974, he was over the concession stand for all camps. He did not let his affliction hamper him from serving God.

Our three daughters are still serving the Lord that their father taught them to love. Some day on Resurrection morning we shall all be together again.

The Benton Harbor church before remodeling.

The Niles church before remodeling.

The Niles church after completion.

Rev. and Mrs. C. C. Deckard, 1969.

5

WARREN DEBBS EMBERLIN

by Warren D. Emberlin
as told to Noble D. Emberlin

My dad was a farmer who owned a three-room house "with a path" on a 120-acre farm. A hardworking, stern man, Dad only gave instructions once. He said, "Whatever you do, do it right." As a child I thought Dad was too hard, but now I appreciate the lessons I learned in obedience.

As a small child, I decided to start to school before I was old enough. I ran down the road for about one-half mile when my uncle stopped in his new 1918 Dodge touring car and took me home. My mother put me in the underground cellar in total darkness. I screamed until I was delivered. I surely don't ever want to be cast into "outer darkness"!

One very cold morning I awoke to find everyone out at the barn doing chores, leaving me alone. "They shouldn't have left me!" Angrily I decided to run away. I put on my old brown overcoat over my sleepers. With no shoes on, I started down the road in full view of the barn, hoping someone would see me. Soon I decided to return to the warm house and hot breakfast. No more running away!

A short time later my mother was expecting again. I hardly knew all that went on. My mother had a wisdom tooth removed while she was with child and infection set in. When a baby sister was born, my mother's face was so swollen she could barely see the baby. Shortly after the baby died. My mother never got well either, as the infection spread. She died at thirty-nine when I was nine.

When I was ten, my dad took yellow jaundice and died at forty-one. My uncle, administrator of the estate, sold most of our possessions to pay debts. The family that I lived with showed me much love. My brother went to live with an aunt. Later I lived with my Uncle Elbert, his wife, and two daughters. Then my brother got married so I lived with him. My education continued up to the eleventh grade, all that was available in our area.

Soon after I got out of school I began to date Carmen Ruby Vanderburg. After dating for two years, we married on June 12, 1932. We moved into a two-room house belonging to my wife's cousin, furnished with apple green furniture that I built out of used lumber. In the fall we took a delayed honeymoon, driving a stripped-down Model T Ford to western Oklahoma to pick cotton.

In the early part of 1933 we heard about a Pentecostal revival in Hennipen, Oklahoma, almost seven miles from our place. The evangelists were Brothers Michael, Carley Carter, and M. R. Carter. We took turns with our neighbor, driving his team one night and mine the next. My cousin and I listened outside, then we moved up close.

At the altar call I was surprised when my wife and our neighbor's wife went to the altar. I turned my big, black hat around and around in my hand as I shook uncontrollably. Finally I got a firm hold on the car bumper, but the car shook! Jumping up, I asked my cousin to hold my hat, and I ran to the mourner's bench. Weeping, I repented and felt as if the whole world lifted off me.

Before this my neighbor and I had helped ourselves to a man's horse oats and fed them to our teams on the way home. That night as we neared the field, my neighbor asked, "Are we gonna get some more oats?"

"No, my oat-getting days are over!" I didn't know that the Bible said, "Let him that stole, steal no more," but I did know that my conscience would not let me steal again. Later I was baptized in Eight Mile Creek fed by a cold spring that runs out of the Oklahoma Arbuckle Mountains.

We attended church when we could, as my wife was soon to have our first child. Wanda Mae was born in Sulphur, Oklahoma, on December 6, 1933. She only weighed about three pounds. Her heart stopped, and the nurse had to run to the doctor's car and get a heart pump while the doctor inserted a long needle into the baby's chest. They finally got her breathing. The doctor warned us about having more children since my wife had thirteen convulsions before the birth.

In 1934 the Methodists began a brush-arbor meeting nearby, which we attended. A powerful preacher, the minister preached hard against sin and for the need of restitution. Each night the altar filled with weeping sinners. One fellow got up from the altar, went out, got his horse, and headed for a friend's house. He called the man out and paid him five dollars he had cheated him out of the night before in a poker game. I brought my brother Noble to the altar.

Shortly after this, Brother C. P. Kilgore began a revival

in Hennipen. Signs and wonders followed. Seven out of eight people who were lingering at the arbor saw an angel of the Lord. Five of them were my kinfolks. The next night they tried to tell what they had seen. An angel had appeared, bowed over the pulpit, floated out, caught hold of one of the arbor poles, and then disappeared. They could hardly tell it for weeping. A spirit of weeping spread over the congregation from the tops of our heads to the tip of our toes. To this day when I talk about it, I still can feel the surge of the Spirit like 'possum tracks going up and down my spine, and tears still come to my eyes. Oh, what an experience!

In 1935 we attended a campmeeting in Weewoka, Oklahoma. My wife had some large lumps in her breast so she went on a long fast. One night there was a prayer line and my wife got in it. When she was prayed for, she received the Holy Ghost and the Lord healed her. The lumps were completely gone! I received the Holy Ghost in July of 1935 in Elmore City in Brother Kilgore's revival.

In 1936 while we were living just out of Katy, Oklahoma, Wanda, who was about two years old, became very ill. We had no telephone, no car, and no neighbors. The church was about six miles away. Desperately I went outside under the stars and called on the Lord. He told me to anoint Wanda with oil and pray. We only had some Fitch hair oil so I used that. When we finished praying, she fell asleep, and when she awoke she asked for water. She drank it and was all right. Praise God!

In 1938 when Wanda was five, she was sitting on a bench by a wood heater when she fell into the heater, burning her legs badly. Quickly we took her to our pastor's home in Hennipen. Brother and Sister Carter and

Brother and Sister W. O. McComb were in revival there so we all prayed. Wanda screamed with pain. As we prayed, she suddenly stopped screaming and started to play with the other children. God had taken away the pain.

About a week or so later, she began to swell so we took her to the hospital in Winnie Wood. The doctors were upset because we hadn't brought her in at first. They treated the burns but said she would never walk again because of the damage. But thank God for His touch!

While Wanda was still in the hospital, I hitchhiked home for service. That evening Brother Carter asked me to preach. I had felt the Lord dealing with me to preach but had not obeyed. I preached from Exodus, "When I see the blood I will pass over you." That began my preaching ministry.

Shortly after my first message, Wanda was released from the hospital but was not walking. A few days later when my wife was outside, she heard Wanda screaming. She ran into the house to find that Wanda had gotten out of bed and walked across the room. She has walked ever since.

I preached on street corners, in schoolhouses, tents, brush arbors, open-air meetings, churches, and Bible conferences. For about eight years I evangelized. I received my first ministerial certificate in 1939 and was ordained in 1940 with the Pentecostal Assemblies of Jesus Christ. Later I received my ordination certificate with the United Pentecostal Church.

When Wanda began school, we moved to Elmore City, where Brother Parkey was our pastor. When I wasn't preaching, I worked as a roofer, which helped us through hard times. Once I was flat broke, so I left home and went to another town to find work. I went to tell my pastor, and as I was leaving, he handed me forty-five cents. "I don't need this," I said.

"Take it. We'll be here at home and won't need it," he said.

I hitchhiked to another town, found a house that had shingles missing in front, and went to inquire about replacing them. I had to wait for the man of the house. At first he said, "No, I'll do it myself." As I turned to leave, he said, "Wait. What will you charge beside board?" "Two dollars," I answered. I got the job. I slept out in the back yard, took my meals with them, and made $2.50. Then he got me another job.

When I had made ten dollars, I went to the bus station and bought a ticket to Oklahoma City. I got my brother-in-law and sister-in-law and we came back to work and rented a place to live. We worked for several days, then went to Elmore City for my family. "I've got to go by Brother Parkey's to pay my tithes," I said. My brother-in-law said, "Wait, take him my tithes too." We went back to work and I bought a Chevy car for thirty dollars, then we returned to Elmore City. Our son, Jerry David, was born there on July 4, 1941. The doctor charged me five dollars.

During our time in Elmore we met a tall, young trinitarian preacher, James L. Gilbert. Brother Parkey and I set out to win him over to the Jesus Name message. With God's help, he saw the light and soon began preaching Jesus. He spent time in our home, and we went on several preaching journeys together.

One cold winter we wanted to go to a conference in Tulsa. Someone had given us some pecans that still had outer hulls. I soaked them in water, hulled them, and sold them for conference money. We stayed in an unheated trailer home, but the Lord richly blessed us.

Another time we hitchhiked to Savoy, Texas, to a fellowship meeting, finally catching a ride with Brother Bingham. By the time we arrived, he had a carload of folks he had picked up, some even riding the hood.

Brother James met a young lady, Ruth Weaver, in our church whose dad let them come only to our house on their dates. Later they married. Years later their oldest son married our younger daughter.

In 1943 we went to California to work and preach. We preached in LaMont for Brother Paul Winters of the Pentecostal Assemblies of the World. We worked in Wasco, where I heard about some Jesus Name folks meeting in a house. I preached for them several times, then I located an empty building for rent for thirty-five dollars. The next service I asked, "Would you like me to rent it?" They agreed and our first service was packed out. Soon I reorganized the Sunday school, ordered material from a Christian publishing house, and appointed a woman teacher. Then I organized the books, and soon we had some good musicians and singers.

While we lived in Wasco my three-year-old son, Jerry, came in the house one day asking for a drink. "Just a minute," my wife said. A jar of kerosene was on the floor. Thinking it was water, Jerry drank it and became violently ill. I came home from work and we began to pray. I got him into the car, praying as I drove. Then I asked, "Do you want a milkshake?" I got it and he never lost it. God heals!

We preached in Strathmore in a storefront for nine nights. The pastor closed the meeting without taking up any offerings. After service, a backslidden preacher who had prayed back through got up on the altar bench and said, "I think we need to take up the preacher an offering." I got about nine dollars.

I preached a revival for Brother Rode in Modesto. One night as I was preaching, a man and a woman walked in with Bibles. They came to the altar and prayed. Afterward they said that they were Nazarene, had been to their service, and were walking by when they looked in and saw me. Previously they had dreamed about a man preaching and that man was I. So they came in and heard the truth.

While in Modesto, Wanda was riding in the back of our pickup. When I stopped at a light, she slid back against the tailgate, which came open, and fell to the ground in front of an eighteen-wheeled truck. Thank God, he stopped.

We preached a revival in a home missions church for Brother Andie Evans in Tracey. Then we preached Brother Ike Terry's first revival in Bakersfield. We preached several revivals for Brother H. Greggs in Safford. After coming to Denison, we were invited to preach the eleventh Arizona prayer and Bible conference in May.

In 1949 while we were in Elmore City, several men told us we ought to go to Springer and help the people there as they had no leader or building. I decided to investigate and drove to see Brother D. B. Black, the one in charge. His wife said, "He's not here; he's in Ardmore."

"Let's go to Ardmore [a town of twenty thousand] and park on the main street," I decided. "The first man I meet will be Brother Black." That's exactly what happened! I felt I was in the will of God to go to Springer. We drove back and forth to the services from our home in Elmore. Sometime later we decided to move the church to Ardmore. Several wanted to move but others wanted to stay. Some went but some stayed.

We purchased two corner lots in the southeast part of town. When we were ready to build, the city informed us that we could not build a church within three hundred feet of any adjoining property. The neighbors passed a petition signed by all the homeowners complaining that we made too much noise. So we sold the property at a profit and moved.

Brother Black owned some commercial property and he deeded the lot on the back of it for a church. We built a church facing Palmer Street, a very narrow street connecting E and F streets. We didn't have many men while we were building, so the ladies helped. Sister Emberlin and Sister Edith James helped pull up the rafters with a rope, then we nailed them. Brother Black, men who were just passing through town, and I built most of the building.

Night and day we worked, especially Brother Black. His family got low on groceries. The children thought this was strange because they were used to plenty, but the Lord carried them though. After the birth of their baby, Sister Black got very sick. The doctor said she would not improve, but when we prayed, she improved, got up, and cooked breakfast the next day.

We had to take baptismal candidates fifty miles to Sister Miller's church in Gainsville, Texas, for baptism. At our opening service, the place was packed with Oklahoma District officials, pastors, saints, and friends. Holy Ghost rain fell inside, and natural rain fell on the outside. We stayed at Ardmore about a year.

In 1951 I preached in Denison, Texas, for Brother F. C. Smith, who had begun a work in a storefront and was beginning a building. When Brother Smith decided to leave, he called me to try out for the church. I was very content so I told him, "No, I'm not coming to preach because they already know how strict I preach."

They held a vote anyway and he called, "It was one hundred percent!" I was still not willing so I said, "I'll let you know." On my way to Durant, Oklahoma, for a service, I told my wife, "I must let Brother Smith know something. If the first station in town has a telephone, I'll stop and call. It's unlikely he'll be home." As I rolled into town the first station had a phone so I called. He was home and I said, "I'll come."

We left Ardmore for Denison. We finished the church building, then finished the parsonage.

Our Romona Kay was the first baby born in Grayson County so we received a write-up in the paper and free merchandise. We organized a Sunday school and offices in the church, then started planning an educational building.

The state decided to build an embankment for a highway right in front of our church, hiding us from the highway and causing water to run in front of our property. We took our case to court but the state won, so we decided to move.

We purchased property one block south of Highway 69 and one block east of 75. We bought five lots with a two-story house for a parsonage. We moved our auditorium to the new location and had services for a good while.

We had a revival with Curtis, Simeon, and Dorothy Young in the old building, also a great revival with Joe Ben Terry and Jack DeHart. Many soldiers from nearby Perrin Air Force Base received the Holy Ghost and new families moved in.

In February 1953 our daughter Wanda married William C. Gray. They evangelized for a while, then pastored in Longview, Texas, and Kansas City, Missouri. They have two married sons, Rodney and Nathan, who are active in the church in Denison. Wanda and her husband are now in the church in Denison.

In 1959 we began our new church, a 44-by-84 block building attached to the old building, which is now used for education.

When I was in my forties, I got the childhood disease of mumps and was sick unto death. In addition we had some church problems that added stress. Sister Cora McCray prayed the prayer of faith and the Lord lifted me up!

Our son, Jerry, married Judy Cravens in Durant, Oklahoma, in 1959. They had two sons. The first child, Monty, died at two and a half. Later Jonathan David was born to carry the Emberlin name.

In 1971 we sent our younger daughter to Texas Bible College. All the children went to Bible college—Wanda to Tulsa, Jerry to Stockton, California, and Kay to Texas. Kay married David Gilbert, and they evangelized for eight years.

In 1978 my wife was selling peanut brittle at Christmas when she accidentally locked the keys in her car and had to walk home. As she crossed a street, the light changed and a car hit her, injuring her severely. She spent three months in the hospital. We were under so much pressure that I called my son-in-law to help with the church. My wife improved and began to walk again, then in December 1980 she had a heart attack and a stroke, which paralyzed her left side. My son-in-law agreed to stay on as co-pastor. Then in 1983 my wife had another stroke.

We had a lot of hard times, so I retired and my son-in-law became pastor. Since he became pastor, the congregation has built an educational building and remodeled the auditorium. Souls have been saved and the church is growing.

I still minister some here and preach out when I am called. The Lord has blessed. I didn't keep complete records of the folks we baptized when we first came to Denison, but according to the records we have and my memory, we have baptized over five hundred. Several ministers have gone out of this church. Among them are Robert Molsbee, Gulfport, Mississippi; Rodger Hennigan, Bogalusa, Louisiana; John Brooks, evangelist; Alan Dorries, Ardmore, Oklahoma; and Royce Robinson, Valient, Oklahoma.

Since my retirement I started metal detecting. While in a schoolyard, a young man asked me to look for a ring. The tone sounded, so I knelt to dig. The young man hit the back of my head intending to rob me. I swung my detector. He ran! I thanked God I could defend myself.

In my younger days I claimed Psalm 67:2 and asked God for "saving health," and the Lord has given me exactly that. Two other verses—Psalm 71:9, 18—have also been a great comfort to me. Thank God for experiences; they bring hope!

Church on Bells Drive.

Remodeled church. The Denison *Herald* carried a later picture of the First Pentecostal Church in January 1962.

The Emberlin family in 1953, left to right: Jerry, Bro. Emberlin, Kay, Wanda, Sis. Emberlin.

Rev. and Mrs. W. D. Emberlin, 1984.

6

ORVILLE T. FRAME

by Ilene K. Dewar

On January 1, 1901, at Topeka, Kansas, the Holy Spirit was poured out at a Bible school directed by Charles F. Parham. This new spiritual movement was still in its infancy when on August 21, 1902, a son was born to Van Meter and Mary Frame in Wayne County, Indiana. The Frames named their baby Orville T. Frame, a name that in later years became synonymous with Pentecost around Bloomington, Indiana.

Soon after Orville's birth, the Frames moved to the northeastern Indiana farming community of Lynn in Randolph County. There Mr. Frame and his seven sons worked long, hard hours in the fields. The Frames' daughter died in early childhood.

Because the farm needed so much attention, few boys had the opportunity to complete formal education. Orville's schooling ended with the eighth grade. Although he regretted his lack of education, Orville Frame did not allow it to hinder him from working for the Lord. Instead, he spent his life learning how to apply God's Word in his own life as well as in the lives of many people he contacted over more than a half century of ministry in Bloomington.

Life was more than farm chores and hard work, however, and the godly influence of his dear Quaker mother always inspired Orville. He often spoke of the love and wisdom of a godly mother who helped shape his character.

Because he could not find work in Lynn in 1920, Orville moved to Bloomington, where he and his brother Ellis both worked at the Showers Brothers Furniture Factory. Two houses up from where the Frame boys stayed, lived Bennett and Laura Lane and their teenage daughter, Alice Jane. Soon Orville began to court her.

On their dates, they attended a Holiness mission on the corner of Twelfth and Indiana where Grover Hawkins preached. One night as Hawkins was preaching, God revealed the true plan of Bible salvation to him. He was baptized in Jesus' name and filled with the Holy Ghost. Alice's parents attended this church.

On a cold, rainy Sunday, March 19, 1922, after a two-year courtship, Homer Smith, founder and pastor of the Pentecostal Faith Assembly, united the nineteen-year-old Orville T. Frame and fifteen-year-old Alice Jane Lane in marriage in her parents' home. After the wedding, despite the heavy rainstorm, Orville's father drove the young couple to their new home east of Bloomington. "There wasn't any money for a honeymoon, but we were excited because we were being driven to our new home in a buggy pulled by an old gray horse." Three children were born to this union: Hubert, Mary Francis, and William. There are eight grandchildren and nine great-grandchildren.

In the early days of their marriage, Orville had to walk to work at the factory for six dollars a week. Rent was fifteen dollars a month and pork chops eight cents a pound.

The services they attended planted seed that grew. The Frames knew they needed God. At the factory Orville and a co-worker began to talk about the Jesus Name doctrine sweeping the country. They decided to study the Scriptures to prove this doctrine false. But when O. T. Frame, with a Quaker background, and his friend, with a Church of Christ background, began to study the Bible earnestly, the Word convinced them that Jesus is God and that they needed Him. Later in his ministry, Brother Frame often counseled those who were confused about the Oneness doctrine to search the Scriptures themselves.

Charles Bohall pastored the Twelfth and Indiana mission where Orville and Alice attended. The small congregation had to vacate the mission site, moved from place to place, and finally began home prayer meetings. At one of these cottage prayer meetings in the home of the Ralph Johnsons, the Frames repented and were baptized on March 6, 1926. Two weeks later they both received the Holy Ghost. Later Brother Johnson became a board member in Brother Frame's church and also preached the gospel. According to some who were at the prayer meeting, Brother Frame received the Holy Ghost while lying on the floor. Quite a contrast from his Quaker upbringing!

From that day, Orville Frame was Pentecostal, yet some of the Quaker ways instilled in him always remained ingrained in his life. Seldom did Brother Frame shed tears in public, yet heaven has the record of the copious amount of private tears he shed in almost fifty-eight years in the ministry. His faith in God reached a depth that most of us long for, but it was a very personal, private matter with him. He never spoke of the struggles or the battles he had; he just found better ways to minister through trials. He listened a lot but spoke little.

Because of his ill health, Brother Bohall persuaded Orville to speak occasionally. One elderly man remembers his first sermon. Brother Frame paced back and forth across the platform several times and about five minutes later said, "That's all there is," and sat down. This first sermon was hardly a foretaste of the fine messages Brother Frame preached a little later. My mother recalls going to the "old church across the street" and not getting near the building for the crowds. Finally her father lifted her to his shoulders, but she still could not see the tall, blond, handsome preacher who so captivated his audience. His voice rang out loud and clear. "In the summer with windows open, he could be heard all over the hill."

Brother Bohall's health continued to fail and he resigned, leaving the church with Brother Frame. The congregation met in a room over the Beman-Davis store on Bloomington Square. Later, this group and the saints from the church at Eleventh and Adams streets combined. Ordained in 1928, Brother Frame agreed to preach until they found a pastor.

In 1929 the stock market crashed, plunging the nation into the Great Depression, one of the darkest periods of its history. These humble Pentecostal believers could not afford to pay a pastor, so Brother Frame stayed on for the next fifty-seven years. For the first ten years Brother Frame received no salary from the church. In 1938 the church became large enough for him to give up his job at Showers Factory to be full-time pastor. At this time his salary from the furniture factory totaled about $165 for one year. His first salary from the church was whatever was left after bills were paid. Later he received fifteen dollars a week. Occasionally a couple would give him a dollar or so for a wedding ceremony.

Homer Smith, whose wife later worked faithfully at the Apostolic Bible Institute in St. Paul, built the original Pentecostal Faith Assembly, a thirty-by-sixty-foot wood frame building located across the street from the present structure. Surrounded by vacant lots and a network of dirt lanes leading to small one- or two-room houses, the church sat in an area called Pigeon Hill populated by very poor people. Many of these poor people came to the Pentecostal Faith Assembly and found salvation for their souls. A few are still living and serving God today. At least three men who lived there as teenagers got saved and are pastoring churches in Indiana.

By the early 1930s the congregation grew to 125 and needed a bigger building. But men were out of work and families could not even provide food and shelter, let alone finance a new church. Nevertheless in 1934 Brother Frame designed a new church seating eight hundred and purchased lots across the street for four hundred dollars. Construction began in 1936 and the first service was held in May of 1937.

Finding the money in 1936 for this size of a building was almost impossible. Most of the congregation were widows or women whose husbands did not attend. These women raised most of the money by having bake sales, making and selling quilts, and serving church suppers. Often the sisters would meet together one day and make candy. The next day they would sell the candy, taking in perhaps five or six dollars. Others gave nickels and dimes, which seemed like a fortune.

During construction, Brother Frame worked days at

the factory then went to the church site to work. The few men who attended did all of the work, most of it by hand. Brother Frame dug the basement out with a pick and shovel using a wheelbarrow to cart out the rocks. Occasionally a neighbor man who did not attend helped with the building. Forty years later he accepted Christ. Despite all this hardship, there never has been a mortgage on Pentecostal Faith Assembly.

After working twelve to fourteen hours a day, Brother Frame often came home to a dinner of water gravy and potatoes. Once he found his supper of fried potatoes spilled on the floor when the prop fell out from under the kitchen stove.

It is impossible for church members to know how busy their pastor is in the course of a day. But one Thursday night Bible study, the people got a glimpse of what a day in the life of their pastor was like. As Brother Frame stepped to the pulpit he looked exhausted. He said, "Saints, if I don't make much sense tonight, it's because I had a wedding this morning at nine, a funeral at ten, a wedding at two, a funeral at three, and a wedding at five, and now here we are at Bible study. So if I begin our study with 'Dearly beloved, we are gathered together,' don't think anything of it."

A busy pastor may also occasionally be plagued with lapses of memory. On August 22, 1942, Brother Frame forgot his schedule. That day Brother Frame was scheduled to perform my parents' wedding ceremony; instead he had gone fishing. When he returned, he found a most anxious young couple. He asked, "Shall I change my clothes or do you want to go ahead with the ceremony?" "Let's just go ahead with the ceremony," they decided.

This same scenario was repeated at my aunt and uncle's wedding. Again Brother Frame forgot and when he got home he found Alice Dewar and Reverend John Bault waiting.

Brother Frame's ready smile, hearty laugh, and firm handshake influenced Bloomington and beyond, touching countless lives. He performed 800 wedding ceremonies, conducted approximately 1,300 funerals, and recorded 1,400 baptisms. (Records were not kept in his early ministry.)

His community honored Brother Frame with several plaques for his service. Several Bloomington mayors honored the Frames including Mayor Tom Lemom in 1958, Mayor Mary Alice Dunlap in 1963, and Mayor Frank McClosky in 1978 at the fiftieth anniversary and homecoming services. Also on June 26, 1978 the Frames received a plaque from the Commission on Aging.

During almost fifty-eight years of Brother Frame's ministry, the church enjoyed many wonderful revivals with different evangelists. The late Ben Bonney preached one of the early revivals in the old church and returned for meetings in the new church. Evangelist Tommy Stephen preached one of the first revivals in the new church, during which ninety people were baptized. J. C. Bishop, Kenneth Dyson, Gerald Mangun, the Nelson brothers, W. E. Gamblin, Winston Thomas, Lyndal Krause Whitt, Louise Potter, the Young family, the Kinzie evangelistic party, T. L. Craft, George Glass, the Pasleys, and many others preached there.

The loyalty and hard work of a faithful pastor's wife contributed greatly to Brother Frame's ministry. In the old church, Sister Frame taught the ladies' Bible class.

Later she taught the young people's class several different times. She helped in choir work and provided music for funerals. She began the Ladies Auxiliary and through this organization raised funds for the new church.

In December 1946, Brother Frame began a radio ministry that is still on the air over forty years later. Until five years ago the broadcasts were live each Sunday morning. Now the choir tapes the broadcast for replay on Sunday.

Many men and women under Brother Frame's ministry answered the call to the work of God. They include Lawrence Brown, Robert Cavaness, Michael Douglas, Jim Engledow, the late John Fleener Sr., James Frye, Don Gardner, Leonard Hamm, Will Henderson, Herbert Hogatt, Frank Jackson, Ralph Johnson, Michael Noel, Tracy Noel, Wallace Owings, Neal Pedro, Jamie Shepherd, Robert Sparks, James Wampler, Benton Wright Jr., and Ilene K. Dewar. In 1976 Brother Michael Douglas, one of the home boys, returned from teaching at Western Apostolic Bible College to serve as assistant pastor, a position he held until 1985.

Blessed, happy times filled Brother Frame's life, but times of great sadness and grief came also. One such time involved five young men of the church who had gone duck hunting. Their boat capsized and three of them drowned. Brother Frame preached a triple funeral that sad day.

According to a newspaper clipping, Brother Frame also preached the "loneliest funeral ever held in Monroe County." The headless, desecrated body of Henry Evans Scott was found on an area farm. The only ones attending the graveside funeral were two grave diggers, two funeral directors, a newspaper reporter, and Brother Frame.

Robert Harrell, the funeral director, disturbed by the lack of concern of the family, went into the garden of the funeral home and picked an armful of flowers, which he placed on the plain gray casket provided by the township.

Brother Frame loved children. They seemed to love him even though he had very large hands and towered over them. Yet it was those hands, his twinkling eyes, and great booming laugh that made not only the little ones, but all the congregation, feel safe and secure. Never too busy, he often stopped to listen to a child who shyly ventured up to this giant of a man.

One Sunday morning when he made a rare visit to the Junior Sunday school department, one of the awestruck boys asked, "Does the O. T. in your name stand for Old Testament?" With a twinkle in his eye and a broad grin, Brother Frame said, "No, son, I think it stands for old-timer."

When my sister was a child, she said, "Mom, do you know what I think God looks like?" Since my sister had shown little interest in church, Mom wondered about her theory. Kathy's response was, "I think God looks just like Brother Frame." Brother Robert Cavaness declares he had the same thought as a young man.

Hours of grief, sleepless nights, and buckets of tears filled the private life of this very public man who cared for his flock so long. In public, however, he never preached his feelings, something he cautioned young ministers against. He faithfully preached the Word.

In the twilight years when the golden locks of unruly hair turned to gray, his once proud, sure steps became an unsteady shuffle, the twinkle in his eye dimmed, and the once big, booming voice faded to a whisper, the heart of this shepherd still tenderly cared for his sheep. Just one day before he was admitted to the hospital for the final time, he preached his last sermon. His strength was almost gone and he began to sway. Someone jumped to catch him but he regained his balance, stayed on his feet, and finished that last message to his people.

On November 5, 1985, O. T. Frame went home to be with the Lord. Of great men many things can be written, yet it is hard to tell the whole story without the clutter of too many flowery, unnecessary words and phrases.

What then can be said of O. T. Frame? He was faithful, and he led God's people by God's Word through good times and bad, through days of the Depression, through years of war into times of prosperity. A kind man, a just man, a temperate man, a wise and gentle man. Eternity alone records the good that this man accomplished in his eighty-three years of life.

Pentecostal Faith Assembly, Bloomington, Indiana.

Rev. and Mrs. Orville
Frame

Rev. and Mrs. Orville Frame, June 1972.

Orville Frame and the brethren.

Bloomington church

7

WALTER S. GUINN

by Jane Guinn McClain

Walter S. Guinn was a man who wore many hats in his lifetime. He was a pastor, an evangelist, a Bible teacher, a husband, a butcher, and my daddy!

In a small farmhouse in Lincoln County, Missouri, on December 5, 1904, a frail, sickly baby was born. He was named Walter Sampson Guinn. His mother was a godly woman who shouted down the aisles of the Christian Church and walked in all the light she had. She was afraid she would not live to raise her son due to her weakened condition. So as she lay in her bed holding her new baby, she asked God to take care of them. Suddenly a man appeared in the window. He told her he had brought her a message from the Lord. He said that God had His hand on her baby and that He was going to take care of both of them. Grandma Guinn felt surely she had seen an angel from the Lord.

When Walter was still a young child, the family moved to St. Louis. He gave his heart to the Lord when he was a child about the age of twelve. As a teenager he drifted away from the church, but my grandma held on to that promise she had received when he was born.

By eighteen Walter had become a butcher and was managing a meat market. One day a young girl came into the market to buy meat, and she caught his eye. She kept coming back, as it seemed she was receiving more meat per pound than others did. Stella Frazier had just moved to St. Louis from the mountains of Kentucky and knew nothing of Pentecost. But God had a plan.

On September 25, 1923, Stella became Mrs. Walter Guinn. Right away my grandmother started telling Stella about the Lord, and she took her to church with her. On Christmas Day, 1924, my mother was baptized and filled with the Holy Ghost at Benjamin Harrison Hite's church. On the same night my sister, Margie (Mrs. Robert McFarland), was dedicated to the Lord at the age of one month. Now my grandmother had someone to help her pray for her son.

After becoming so miserable (prayer works that way), Walter Guinn finally came to church. With the Spirit of the Lord drawing him, he headed for the altar. As he wrestled with the Lord, his body was bounced around like a rubber ball. Someone who was there told me that my daddy's body raised about three feet off the floor. Finally the words "anytime, any place, anywhere" flowed from his mouth. He completely surrendered, God filled him with the Holy Ghost, and he had his calling.

My dad preached his first sermon the very next night in a storefront mission on Broadway in St. Louis. Often God will call someone to preach and send him elsewhere, but in the case of Walter Guinn, he started in north St. Louis and finished in north St. Louis. But his life touched the lives of thousands of people all over the country.

When my folks started to work for God, all they had or needed was the Bible, a tambourine, and the Spirit of the Lord. God took it from there!

My dad always said he was a pole and line fisherman for Jesus. He said when you fished this way, you catch one fish at a time and you know what you have. He did not go in for "big campaign" preaching. He called this net fishing. You get a net full, but you never know exactly what you have. So one by one my dad built his congregation.

The first church building we worshiped in was on Sullivan Avenue. Here hoodlums threw brickbats through the windows. Persecution, however, gave the old saints the foundation that they needed to stand later.

I guess my daddy was best known in the St. Louis area for his tent meeting every summer on the corner of Fourteeth and Branch streets. There are people today who come by the church and say they heard him preach in the tent. For years many people who belonged to no particular church called for Daddy to preach funerals and perform weddings because they remembered the tent meetings.

Of course preacher's kids look at things from a different slant than most people. My memories of the tent meetings are somewhat different. I remember being awakened in the middle of the night and rushed out in a thunderstorm to head for the tent. The ropes that held the tent had to be loosened and then tightened during the rain to keep the tent from blowing away, and all hands were needed.

My dad had kept his job at the meat market, as times were hard and he needed his salary to help pay church expenses. He would buy day-old bread for two cents a loaf and other bakery goods, and pile up the baked goods on the back seat at the church on Tuesday night Bible study. After church all the saints would take as much as they needed for their families. Daddy would laugh and say that was one way to get folks out to Bible study.

As the church grew so did the need for Daddy to be there full time. But he just could not give up the security of his job. One day my sister, Margie, took very sick. The doctor said he thought she would die. Daddy told the Lord if He would heal Margie that he would give up his job and trust the Lord for every need. Immediately Margie was healed. From that day until the day he died, I never did know my dad or my mother ever to use a credit card. They trusted the Lord, and if they did not have cash for something, they did not buy it.

Although Daddy ended his career as a butcher we always assured him that it would come in handy later because we will need a butcher to kill the fatted calf at the marriage supper in heaven.

One summer while we were in the tent meeting, our church building was sold. We wondered if we would have to stay in the tent all winter, but the Lord provided a building for us. The building stood at the corner of Blair and Warren streets and was located in a shopping district called The White Way. So we called our church The White Way Tabernacle. It seemed to fit us.

It was at this church that the plans were worked out for the merger between two large Pentecostal organizations, The Pentecostal Assemblies of Jesus Christ and The Pentecostal Church, Incorporated. Daddy was the last pastor who invited the board of the P.A. of J.C. to use our church and our home. It was a historical occasion.

Now, here again is that "preacher's kid" version of this historical event. My mother was called away from home due to the death of her father. I was fifteen years old, and now I was the lady of the house. I was in charge of entertaining all of those preachers as well as some of their wives.

For the first few days I really had a problem. I would make coffee for some and then hurry and hide the pot and make tea for others. I had to get Coca-Cola for some, then arrange for grape or orange soda for those of a different persuasion. Finally I told my daddy we had to do something. I did not want to offend anyone, but enough was enough. As always, the wisdom of Solomon came from my daddy. We decided to put everything on the table, pray over it, and let everyone's conscience be his guide.

In his early ministry my dad had gone back to his birthplace in Lincoln County to preach. Later he went to Troy, Missouri, and started a church. Now it is a growing church. My brother, Eddie Guinn, pastored this church for years until he came to St. Louis to help Daddy in the church.

Some of the original saints had come from near Vichy, Missouri. They encouraged Daddy to start a church for their family back home. So with the help of the saints at our church, a new work was established at Vichy, Missouri. It is still an active church today.

Times changed and many of our people moved farther out to the suburbs. The church followed them and located at the corner of Grand and Carter. Since we had left the old White Way shopping district behind, we changed the name of the church to Northside Pentecostal Church.

About this time Dad put on the hat of a teacher. He

was asked to teach a class at the Gateway College of Evangelism. Oh, how he enjoyed this! God had given him so much knowledge of the Scriptures that his greatest joy was giving it back to young people in his classes.

He taught in many Bible conferences, and he always kept his charts handy when anyone would call. Of course, the caller always got two for one, for my mother was always ready to go with him. She never let an opportunity pass when she could tell everyone about the Ladies Auxiliary work for the state of Missouri, of which she was the leader. One of the highlights of their year was going to Bogalousa, Louisiana, for the Bible conference.

In 1969-70 Dad and my brother, Eddie, built a new church in north St. Louis County on Shepley Drive, where they served as co-pastors. Dad's health had begun to fail and the load was just too heavy for him to carry alone.

In the last year of his life Bible teaching became very important to him. As a youth project at the church, the youth taped his last Bible studies. He didn't have the strength to stand to teach, but he sat in a chair and made it all the way from Creation to Revelation. Sometimes his voice got a little weak, but with those tapes he has continued to preach the truth to us even though he has been gone for many years.

In the last few weeks of his life he suffered several strokes. The doctors did not want us to keep him at home because they thought he would be in too much pain. But he wanted to be at home, so that is where he was. Every day I would ask him if he was in pain, and every day the answer would be the same, "No, that is my miracle."

On December 31, 1979, at the age of seventy-five Daddy left us.

A leader to the end, he was the first of our family to cross to the other side. But he left happy memories and a desire for the rest of us to follow. For over fifty years he had pastored one church and one congregation in one town, and I never heard a man say anything bad about him.

What more could a daughter ask!

Walter S. Guinn, 1904 - 1979.

Stella Guinn, first Ladies Auxiliary leader for Missouri.

Rev. and Mrs. Walter S. Guinn

Walter S. Guinn preaches the Word.

80

8

GEORGE WASHINGTON HAMILTON

written for Mary Adele Hamilton
by LaJoyce Martin

He was known as "The Weeping Prophet" even before he accompanied Roy to the electric chair.

A lady whom he pastored reports that he came to the hospital to pray for her, stood silently at her bedside with bowed head, then turned and walked away. On the floor was a pool of tears. She was healed.

But now we are getting ahead of Mary's story!

Mary Adele Hamilton started a biography of her husband's life but suffered a stroke before she was able to complete the last three chapters of the book. This is her story, condensed and rephrased.

George Washington Hamilton, the last of eight children, was orphaned soon after his birth on August 14, 1909. Shifted from sister to brother, aunt to uncle, sorely in need of love and guidance, he felt he was a misfit everywhere.

George's oldest brother was murdered, leaving a young widow and two small fatherless children. Not old enough to be heard, George listened in silence as the stabbing was discussed, pro and con. It was the talk of the town. He quietly formed his own verdict and pledged his own method of retaliation. Revenge rankled in him, tormented him!

Night after night, he nourished that resolution and grew bitter. At the trial, when the murderer was not convicted, it became George's sole responsibility to settle the score. The crime would not go unavenged, regardless of what the law had ruled!

At an early age, George left his hometown to make his own way in life. Youth and inexperience forced him into the most common fields of labor. Being alert and physically strong, he found jobs with construction companies, railroad workers, and oil field laborers.

Although he was mentally occupied and away from the scene that constantly reminded him of the offense, the feeling of revenge still simmered underneath. He still had a matter to settle back home—some day. He wasn't forgetting that!

At last, in 1932, George returned to his hometown, now in his early twenties. He met some old friends who invited him to a Pentecostal meeting in progress "upstairs in the old feed store building." A bit reluctant to go, he was surprised to find it entirely different from what he had expected. He was heartily welcomed and treated as a friend!

The next night he went back; he actually wanted to go! It was there again—the friendliness and sincerity. And how those people sang! And what was this portion of Scripture the preacher was reading? Was it really in the Bible? "Dearly beloved, avenge not yourselves, but rather give place unto wrath: for it is written, Vengeance is mine; I will repay, saith the Lord" (Romans 12:19).

Now who told the minister about his plans of revenge? How did he know? George was deeply stirred and resolved to look more carefully into the matter.

He had heard that a little book was kept in the pulpit with names of those for whom these devoted people were praying. He had an overwhelming desire to see that book, so the following night he mingled among these friendly people, working his way toward the front. He saw the list, with his very own name near the top, and it touched him profoundly.

He went home and began reading his Bible. At two o'clock George's light was still burning. A few nights later, he was in the altar, and God baptized him with the Holy Ghost. He felt pure, clean, and at peace with God, himself, and everyone! Tears flowed down his cheeks. For the first time in his life, he felt secure, loved, and wanted. Now he had a purpose for living.

That night Brother Frank Martin, assisting Evangelist Powell Sojourner, talked to George about being baptized in water. He had no idea that he meant now—tonight! But being desirous to obey all Scripture, he assented. Since George had brought no clothing for the occasion, Brother Martin attired him in some of his own blue-striped overalls and a work shirt. To a person of less serious attitude, the picture would have been hilarious: five-foot-eight-inch George dressed in the clothes of a man well over six feet tall. The legs of the overalls were rolled up almost to his knees and the sleeves to the elbows, making him resemble a farmer's scarecrow. George put it this way: "I'm sure I must have looked like a rooster with socks on."

Outward appearance was forgotten. That night a

contented young man slept soundly and peacefully in his new-found joy.

But his Pharaoh pursued him! His brother ridiculed, "It won't last. He'll be back for more cigarettes and liquor." His relatives rejected him.

Then George faced the supreme test. As he looked over the congregation one night, observing those who were moved by the Spirit to go to the altar for repentance, he spotted the man who had killed his brother. Here was the man for whom he had carried the torch of revenge for so long! How the devil did his utmost to recapture the freed prisoner! The battle raged. Scalding tears flowed down George's face as he wrestled with his emotions, praying earnestly to God for help. Victory came. George arose from his seat, made his way to the altar, put his arms around his "enemy," and prayed with him for his deliverance. Born in George that night was desire to help fallen humanity find peace with God.

Following this experience, serious-minded George spent long hours in the woods alone, seeking God. He understood that God was dealing with him for a special work, and he desperately cried to God that he might find a way to satisfy the desire to serve which burned in his heart like a flame. He purchased an inexpensive guitar, and with grim determination, practiced and prayed until he mastered at least the fundamentals of the instrument. He began attending nearby revivals, assisting with the music, and singing in such sincere humility that his help was welcomed everywhere.

In March of 1934, a pastor invited George to help in a revival in Dublin, Texas. The evangelist had invited Mary Adele Rhodes along to assist with singing, music, and altar work. They met the first night of the revival. It was not love at first sight, but a romance slowly budded. What attracted the weeping, travailing George to the laughing, light-hearted Mary, no one knew. They were married on Saturday night, September 8, 1934. George borrowed a car and ten dollars to come for Mary, so they started their marriage "deeply in debt."

In November, Mary contacted typhoid fever. Perhaps it was her illness that started the fear in George's heart. For a long time, he had felt his call to preach, but had never mentioned it. A guilty feeling of disobedience plagued him. Uncle John Mounce, a deacon in the pastorless Walnut Springs church, asked George to preach one Tuesday night. Mary was abed with the typhoid fever, and when George returned from service that night, he said, "Guess who preached tonight!" After several missed guesses, he told Mary that he had preached, concluding, "I told them God had called me to preach."

During all of 1935, the couple offered themselves as "helpers" in gospel meetings, anywhere, anytime. They refer to this as their "schooling." In the spring of 1936, George borrowed twenty-five dollars from Mr. Warren, a farmer friend near Gorman, to buy a 1927 Model T Ford, promising to return in the fall and work out the debt in the peanut harvest. By fall, George (nicknamed "Dutch" by all his friends) had launched into the ministry. But true to his word, he returned to Mr. Warren in the fall. Although he was not a Christian, Mr. Warren raised his hand in dismissal, and said kindly, "No, Dutch, you go right on with your preaching and forget the debt. I don't want you to stop your work for God." Years later on December 1, 1957, Brother Hamilton preached Brother

John Warren's funeral and told of this incident.

Near Desdemona, Texas, sat a forlorn-looking school-house called Salem. Brother Hamilton located the man with the key and asked permission to use the building for a revival. The man replied kindly, as if afraid of dampening the spirits of this zealous young preacher, "Young man, I will be glad to give you the key to the building. You are welcome to it, but I don't think anyone will come to hear you preach." Brother Hamilton left with the key in his pocket, elated!

On opening night, a surprisingly large crowd gathered, perhaps rounded up by the sympathetic man with the key. The young couple sang, "That's Why I Love and Adore Jesus" to the tune of "When You and I Were Young, Maggie."

Much to Brother Hamilton's surprise, on the second night of the revival, in walked his brother who had ridiculed him when he received the Holy Ghost. Both brothers wept throughout the service.

One night a teenage boy came to the front with fists clinched. "It's none of your business that I did those things at the party last night, Preacher," his eyes flashed belligerently. Brother Hamilton explained to the young man that he had no knowledge of the party, nor what the boy had done; he was only delivering God's message, as the mailman delivers the mail. The eventful two-week revival was the launching pad for "The Weeping Prophet."

Brother Arthur Clanton with his violin joined them in their next revival, an outdoor affair with a crude platform, located at a downtown intersection in Iredell, Texas. They used a vacant garage next door as lodging for the workers. Singers and musicians poured in from surrounding churches. Brother Clanton preached one night and Brother Hamilton the next. By the end of the week, all the seats were filled, and cars almost blocked the streets.

Garden vegetables were plentiful, but meat was scarce, so Brother Hamilton approached the Lord about the problem. The group found Brother Hamilton driving down five stakes, with strings attached. "What in the world are you doing?" they asked him.

"Fixing these stakes for the five chickens someone is going to bring tonight," he calmly replied. Mysteriously, after service five fryers were attached to the stakes. On another occasion, when they needed bread each of them prayed, and as the bread truck rounded the corner at the intersection, a loaf of bread tumbled off and rolled right toward them!

During a revival at Frankel, a small community of seventy-five to one hundred country folk, Brother Hamilton yelled, "Ma—a—a—ry, come here!" There on the clothesline, where she had hung his only three under-shirts to dry, were just three sets of straps hanging. It was the work of "Satan," a mischievous billy goat. He had eaten the undershirts, all but the straps—a serious situation as they had no money for more!

With a great anointing, Brother Hamilton preached on baptism in the name of Jesus Christ, expecting great results as the altar call was made. No one came. Disappointed and discouraged, he went home and to bed. At two o'clock in the morning he was frightfully jarred to consciousness by a pounding on the door and someone yelling, "Get up, Brother Hamilton!" Hearts pounding, the Hamiltons got up hastily to find two loud Model T cars filled with happy, shouting saints who had brought a young couple for baptism. Revival broke loose!

At the close of a fruitful harvest here, the saints asked Brother Hamilton to stay on as pastor, the five men agreeing to try to raise fifty cents each week to support them. However, they failed to meet their pledge more often than they succeeded. The Hamiltons' son, Jimmy D'Wayne, was born in January of 1937.

Brother Hamilton had made a vow to God to go into virgin territory, and that vow led him to the unreached high plains of Texas. The town was Lamesa, sixty miles south of Lubbock. They were joined by another young couple, Brother and Sister Donald Berry. A visiting evangelist, the Job's-comforter type, said, "You will never build a church in Lamesa." But Brother S. G. McClain, pioneering a work in Lubbock, proved to be a constant tower of strength and courage to the younger ministers. Gradually, a humble twenty-four-by-forty-foot frame building took shape. The building was completed in 1939, when the Hamiltons took over Brother McClain's work in Lubbock for a short duration.

Elder Lewis lived in Bryan, Texas. This dear black minister had been a special inspiration in Brother Hamilton's earliest ministry, and the Hamiltons returned to Bryan for an eagerly anticipated visit. They stayed in the home of Mother Burlin, an aged saint of God who became desperately ill and lapsed into unconsciousness. Hearing the telltale gurgling sound in her throat, Brother Hamilton's faith hit zero, and he sped off frantically in search of Brother Lewis.

Unhurriedly, Brother Lewis gathered up his anointing oil (a concoction of oil and spices he made himself) and his guitar, and at long last was ready to go. Detecting

Brother Hamilton's very obvious anxiety, he placed his hand on Brother Hamilton's arm and said, "Don't you be afraid, Elder Hamilton. God already showed me that Mother Burlin needed help before you ever came."

Undaunted by Mother Burlin's unconscious state, Brother Lewis began strumming his out-of-tune guitar and singing his prayer: "Shake her, Lord! Shake her, Lord!" Still very much unconscious, she began to shake as if she had a Mississippi chill, before everyone's doubting eyes. Turning to her daughter, Brother Lewis said, "Sister, get some house shoes and put them on Mother Burlin, because we're expecting her to come out of this bed!" And come out she did, whirling and spinning like a top!

During this visit, Brother Hamilton took his gun and walked out of town to hunt squirrel. Crawling through a rusty barbed wire fence, he snagged not only his trousers, but his leg also. He thought little of the "minor" injury, assuming it would soon heal, but instead it became red and inflamed and very painful. They loaded up and reached Doucette, Texas, where Brother and Sister Berry were in a revival. By now, Brother Hamilton knew that he was in a serious condition, having become quite ill. Red streaks ran from the angry wound and he had a raging fever and was dizzy. "I think blood poisoning has set in." He sent the naive Sister Hamilton and D'Wayne to church, then turned his face to the wall and prayed like Hezekiah. Immediately a peace settled over him and he fell asleep. He was completely healed.

In Grabo, Louisiana, next on the Hamilton's itinerary, an old French lady rose to testify. Laying her hand over on her sinner husband, she said, "I want you folk to pray for this old man. He's a wicked sinner! He has given me lots of trouble in my life, and for forty years now, I've prayed for God to save him. So far, he is still unsaved, but if he lives another forty years and he is still unsaved, I'll still pray for him."

Embarrassed, Brother Hamilton supposed that the old fellow would get up and leave. When the altar call was given, the old man made his way to the aisle. He's leaving now, thought Brother Hamilton, but to his amazement, the man came stumbling toward the altar, falling to his knees before he got there. He received the Holy Ghost that night, and Brother Hamilton baptized him in Jesus' name.

It was 110 degrees at 10:00 P.M. in August of 1942 when the Hamiltons arrived in Phoenix, Arizona, for a revival. The saints brought along their own air conditioners—a hand fan or song book. After service one night, two ladies got into a fracas, and the older sister, by way of excusing herself of any blame, told Brother and Sister Hamilton, "The rebuke of the Lord came upon me and I came very near slapping her in the name of Jesus!" The Hamiltons were hard put to keep a straight face, and thereafter when church trouble arose they laughingly quoted the "Scripture," but were never quite able to locate it in the Bible.

George Samuel joined the family in 1944 and Robert Dean in 1947. After a season of evangelizing, several short pastorates, and the arrival of these two sons, Brother Hamilton quite unwillingly agreed to take the struggling work in Amarillo, Texas, for thirty days. When revival fires flared, however, that thirty days stretched into nine great years. In 1950 a new church was built. Here, Brother Hamilton served as presbyter for several years, and here Mary Hamilton's fondest wish came true—a beautiful baby girl was born, Georgia Elaine. And here Brother Hamilton met Roy. His niece tells the story:

The Last Mile with Roy

Roy's long arm shot through the prison bars in a warm handshake. He was to die at midnight. As Brother Hamilton turned to leave, he asked, "Are you going home now?"

"No, Roy I'm going with you to the end." It was a promise.

Brother Hamilton had been asked by a relative to visit Roy in the county jail, where he awaited trial in the Forty-Seventh District Court in Amarillo, Texas. The confusing details unscrambled into a sequence of order. After two years of domestic embroilments, in a fit of jealousy and despair Roy took a piece of pipe and bludgeoned his wife, Rachel, to death on April 25, 1951.

Brother Hamilton's first encounter with Roy was unforgettable. Roy, a tall, scholarly-looking man of forty-three, bore closer resemblance to a doctor than a criminal. His open-faced admission to the crime, his honesty, and his genuine remorse shattered Brother Hamilton's professional composure. Roy thanked Brother Hamilton for "a shoulder to cry on." Brother Hamilton, reluctant to become involved for fear of focusing unfavorable attention on the church, felt mysteriously compelled to return to Roy's cell again and again. This was the "first mile" with Roy.

Five months later, the judge pronounced the death

penalty, only the second such sentence ever for Potter County. Brother Hamilton was now on his "second mile" with Roy. To "go with him twain" entailed a personal appearance before the Board of Pardons and Paroles at Austin. He asked that Roy's sentence be reduced to life.

Emblazoned newspaper headlines, "PASTOR JOINS IN PLEA," spotlighted the irony of a defender of right choosing to help a wrongdoer. A cheery little Christmas card from Roy, now in the Texas State Penitentiary at Huntsville, repaid his efforts. It was signed, "Your Brother." He was no longer merely a prisoner, but a mutual friend.

Roy received the Holy Ghost and asked to be baptized in the penitentiary. Brother Hamilton was allowed to fulfill the request in a prison bathtub. The chaplain and warden reported Roy to be one of the best prisoners they had ever had. They were convinced he had obtained pardon from the unseen Judge. Seven months later, the Texas Court of Criminal Appeals affirmed the conviction, with an execution date of February 6, 1953.

When he learned that Roy would be alone, Brother Hamilton made the momentous decision to go the "last mile" with Roy. From that moment on Brother Hamilton slept little. He tossed, he cried, he prayed. He could not eat. It wouldn't be like watching a stranger die; Roy had become a personal friend. His body was behind bars of steel, but his soul was free.

As the end neared, Brother Hamilton knelt and prayed with Roy, whose last request was to be laid to rest beside his wife, Rachel. He assured Brother Hamilton of his own peace with God and unwavering faith in his destiny.

Brother Hamilton entered the execution chamber first

and stood about eight feet directly in front of Roy. Roy's calm last words were, "I have peace and joy in my heart; I love you all and may God bless you." The muffled sounds of a prayer could be heard after the mask was fitted over his face.

For months, Brother Hamilton had prayed for a miracle—new evidence, another appeal, or even a stay of execution. The miracle came, but in a much different way than Brother Hamilton had expected. Roy's body turned a deep purple. Prison authorities felt sure Roy was dead before the initial shock hit his body. The prison physician said that Roy may have "fainted," as indicated by the blood rushing to the surface of his body. The editor and veteran reporter of the *Huntsville Item,* who had covered more than one hundred executions, said he had never witnessed anything like it. Headlines of the *Amarillo Globe Times* blazed this question: "WAS HULEN DEAD WHEN THE CURRENT STRUCK HIM? AUTHORITIES WONDER."

Brother Hamilton turned to walk away. He had gone the "last mile" with Roy. But so had Someone else!

* * * * *

Tender-hearted Brother Hamilton, "The Weeping Prophet," was never the same after this episode. He took a small country church, with no running water or inside bathroom facilities, seeking solace and contrast.

Here the family could hunt and fish and swim in a nearby pond. Here the children could have pets, and when the first stray dog wandered up during the night, he was christened Nicodemus. Here Brother Hamilton says his salary was 400 dollars a month—50 dollars in cash and 350 dollars in peace and quiet! The five wonderful years spent at Mountain Top were a much-needed balm for his weary body and shattered nerves.

There were other churches—Breckenridge and Albany and DeLeon and Coleman and Clarendon and Tahoka and Dumas. The biography begun by Mary Adele Hamilton was abruptly curtailed before their last nine years of successful pastorates in Friona, Texas, and Pauls Valley, Oklahoma, were recorded.

Upon retiring in 1977, Brother Hamilton's lifelong dream was fulfilled at last—to live in Arkansas, where "The Weeping Prophet" still sheds unrestrained tears for his unsaved family and friends.

Rev and Mrs. George W. Hamilton, 1983.

"Dutch" and Adell Hamilton before they married.

Rev. and Mrs. G. W. Hamilton and D'Wayne, 1943.

"Dutch" and Adell at Lubbock Pentecostal Church, 1939.

9

CLIFFORD F. HASKINS

by Wyllis M. Peuse

Clifford Francis Haskins, the third of seven sons, was born in 1905, in Duluth, Minnesota, to Sophia and Arthur Haskins. His father arrived in America from England in 1875 as a thirteen-year-old boy with his parents, Jane and Benjamin Haskins, a Methodist minister.

When Clifford was six, he developed a very high fever and was delirious with pain for days. Finally, in desperation, his mother prayed, "Just take him on, Lord!" After this prayer, she sat down at the pump organ and played "Peace, Be Still." After the song, she noticed that Clifford lay quietly, the fever gone. Although he began to mend, Clifford was very weak, had to learn to walk again, and missed one year of school. Years later, a doctor discovered that his appendix had burst early in life.

Clifford's father became co-owner of a grocery store in Duluth and his teenaged son worked with him. As a young man Clifford had pain in his legs and feet and bound them so that he could work. His family lived one block below the scenic boulevard in Duluth on Eleventh Street. Clifford walked in the wooded area behind their house at sunset calling out to God to heal him.

Clifford's father sang in the Methodist church choir, but his mother attended the Baptist church. At twenty, Clifford went to church with his mother and was baptized. He attended a healing service conducted by Dr. Charles Price in 1926, where he was anointed and prayed for. He related, "I felt the Holy Spirit go through me like an electric current from the crown of my head to the soles of my feet. A man who sat beside me told me about the Holy Ghost, and he took me to a shabby, storefront mission with a potbellied stove and homemade benches. In the apartment overhead, merchants were selling bootleg liquor, which drew a stream of derelicts. God poured out His Spirit in that humble place, as He filled Solomon's Temple."

Clifford returned to the Baptist church to tell the exciting news of Jesus Name baptism and the Holy Ghost. "I've been praying you would not get into false doctrine," the minister said. Clifford never attended the Baptist church again.

Late in November the man invited Clifford back to the mission. "We have an evangelist and his wife who were stage entertainers before their conversion." When they arrived the place was packed.

Clifford later testified, "Although I had never heard about Acts 2:38, I was baptized in Jesus' name the first night. For three nights I prayed earnestly but did not receive the Holy Ghost. I stayed home the fourth night but ran two miles to church the next night. That night, December 1, 1926, about midnight, I received the Holy Ghost and was literally drunk on new wine."

The news of Clifford's experience had an electrifying

effect. One person after another went down in water baptism, many of them coming up out of the water speaking in tongues. "As a sixteen-year-old girl burst out speaking in tongues, I saw a seventy-year-old lady filled with the Spirit too. The Lord began drawing in people from all directions—our fathers, mothers, sisters, brothers, business people, and even men off the lake boats. That revival at 111 North First Avenue West, which started in December of 1926, lasted six months."

Clifford's mother was offended and said, "You're disgracing the family." When Clifford and his younger brother, Wendell, came home late at night singing gospel songs and choruses, their parents marveled at the change in them. Soon Wendell, his three sisters, and a brother-in-law received the Holy Ghost. The night she received the Holy Ghost, Lucile, the nine-year-old sister, prophesied that there would be a great war in Japan. No one took it seriously in 1926 but Clifford remembered it December 7, 1941. Clifford's mother received the Holy Ghost the night she was baptized and was instantly healed of a sinus problem. His father was baptized a few months later.

One night the minister prayed for Clifford's bad cold. An elderly schoolteacher couple were concerned when they saw him lying on the floor of the platform under the power of the Holy Spirit. "Let's find out what sort of spell that young man is under." When he told them that he had received the Holy Ghost, they began seeking it too.

The preacher was David Johnson. "Like our Lord, he was a carpenter but God knew he could trust him to build a temple of 'lively stones' for a dwelling place here on earth. As the revival continued, Brother Johnson and his wife and four small children drew us all close with their dedication, sacrifice and hospitality."

Late in the summer of 1927 the building at 111 North First Avenue West was sold, and the mission moved to an upstairs hall on First Street near First Avenue East. For two years, the mission moved quite often. Then came the stock market crash!

About this time Brother Johnson secured a large well-kept church on the southwest corner of Sixth Avenue and Fifth Street. There the mission developed into an established church. Revival fires swept the congregation. Almost the entire congregation of a church at Mason, Wisconsin, accepted the Apostolic message and came to the Duluth church to be baptized in Jesus' name and to receive the Holy Ghost.

A. D. Urshan came to Duluth and stayed with the Haskins family for a revival in the spring of 1927 at the church at 111 North First Avenue West. Written on the window of the church were the numbers 111 which represented Ephesians 4:5—"One Lord, one faith, one baptism."

Clifford married David Johnson's niece, Helen Marie Johnson, on Thanksgiving, November 24, 1927, at his parents' home. They had one child, Wyllis Marie, born September 28, 1936. A real helpmate, Helen gathered children around her and young couples came to her for help. She worked with the missionary group, sending many gifts of money and clothing to missionaries in all parts of the earth.

In the summer of 1927, the schoolteacher couple invited Clifford to bring the Apostolic message to their neighbors at Lake Nebagamon, Wisconsin. On the third weekend he realized these people had never heard about the Holy Ghost. "God came to my rescue in a most unusual way. Between services the men played ball. An eighteen-year-old came to me at the pitcher's plate. Both his parents had died, leaving him and his sister lonely and destitute. He asked, 'Do you think God would give me the Holy Ghost?' 'Let's pray,' I said. There in the tall grass the Holy Ghost flooded the young man's soul. His best friend begged me to pray for him also.

"Then God opened the understanding of those people to the Apostolic message. That's when Jesus called me into His service and I found a real purpose in life. I baptized those first converts in Jesus' name, and most of them were filled with the Holy Ghost. We had to carry them to the sands of the beach, where they lay speaking in other tongues. Each time I baptized more converts, the vacationers at the lake formed a large semicircle in their canoes to watch.

"Although I was asked to preach many times, I did not seek ordination until 1939 at a ministerial conference at Bishop Johnson's church in Superior."

Clifford loved to sing and play his guitar. Praying at the altar with hungry seekers was his special joy. In 1940 Clifford, Helen, and four-year-old Wyllis moved to Turin, Iowa, where he took the pastorate of a group of people at the request of Elder Alfred Lawrence of St. Paul, Minnesota. In 1942 the draft board contacted thirty-eight year-old Clifford about army service. He gave up the church in Turin and returned to Duluth, telling the officials he was a minister. "What seminary did you attend?" they asked. Finally they accepted his explanation.

The Spooner revival came about through the invitation

of the schoolteacher couple. They had retired from teaching and had concessions in two large office buildings in Duluth where they sold tobacco and confections, sometimes shaking dice to see who would pay. After they received the Holy Ghost, they did not want to sell tobacco and shake dice so in 1945 they moved to a township called Rocky Ridge eight miles from Spooner, Wisconsin, where they began to farm.

They told neighboring farmers about the baptism of the Holy Ghost, which had transformed their lives. Life had been cruel to this family; they had lost two homes and all their possessions by fires. Also their grown son had been crippled by meningitis as an infant, but God had miraculously turned their sorrow into joy and happiness. In the summer of 1934 their neighbors secured the use of the schoolhouse and invited Clifford to tell them about the Spirit.

"When we arrived that Sunday, people packed the schoolhouse to learn more about the Holy Spirit. They begged us to come every Sunday for meetings. The Rocky Ridge revival at Spooner went on for three years.

"At the close of the night service the next Sunday, a man asked to be baptized in Jesus' name, followed by his wife and children. Every Sunday others came. At first only one or two received the Holy Ghost but others hungered.

"The revival gained momentum, and some came from Clear Lake, sixty miles away. Some stopped in after a dance to 'see the show' then returned to become one of those seeking God.

"In this county of small farms a great drought in the Midwestern states from 1934 to 1936 created what became known as the dust bowl. Strong winds raised dust clouds that darkened the sun as far north as Duluth. During this time of utter hopelessness and despair, however, many found their way to that town hall and heard the gospel.

"One destitute family, fearing their children would be taken from them, fled their county and came to Rocky Ridge to our meetings. They reached out to God like a drowning man for a life preserver. The woman was very large, posing quite a problem when we baptized her. Although I had a big, six-foot man helping, we could only get her up on the bank with her legs still in the water when she began speaking in tongues.

"She had a large ten-year-old daughter who also wanted to be baptized one hot Sunday in July 1936. As we drove from Duluth south ninety miles to Spooner, the temperature climbed to 110 degrees at the Spooner town hall. Several people waited outside including the girl. When we got in, she dropped to her knees and began calling on the Lord for the Holy Ghost. She prayed so hard that we feared for her heart in the heat. We tried to persuade her to wait until later that afternoon or night, but she continued seeking the Holy Spirit. Then God heard and filled that hungry heart with the miraculous Holy Spirit.

"My wife, Helen, played the piano until the rafters rang, and my old guitar seemed to sound sweeter than ever to those people as we sang chorus after chorus. One young man played a banjo, another a violin, and a third an accordion. This last man had been one of those who stopped in on his way from a dance. He and his whole family were baptized in Jesus' name and filled with the Holy Ghost. That was the year our daughter, Wyllis Marie, was born, and all those people looked forward to her arrival and rejoiced with us. It was the happiest year of our lives!

"The young burly banjo player had lived a rebellious life, ending up in the penitentiary. Then he came to the meeting and saw real joy. None of us were aware of how hard Satan fought to hold onto him. In the midst of an evening service, the man dropped his banjo, turned on the rostrum, and started beating the wooden wainscoting with his fists until they bled. The people were shocked and stunned, great fear filled their faces. Quietly I placed my hands on him and began to pray for God to calm the tempest in his soul. Soon he was baptized in Jesus' name and filled with the Holy Ghost. Later he married a Spirit-filled girl."

Clifford Haskins became a licensed minister with the Pentecostal Assemblies of Jesus Christ in 1935 and was ordained by the Pentecostal Assemblies of the World in 1939. During the year 1944-45 he held the position of vice-chairman for the Minnesota State Council of the Pentecostal Assemblies of the World.

In 1945 the shipyards where Clifford worked closed and the family moved to Eau Claire, Wisconsin, where he worked for the U.S. Rubber Company. Pastored by Joseph P. Rulien, the church in Eau Claire met in a mission but was building a stone church on the banks of the Chippewa River. The elderly pastor asked Clifford to assist him. Upon his death in 1952 the church elected Richard S. Davis pastor. Before long Brother Davis appointed Clifford as his assistant. In 1957 Clifford became an ordained minister of the United Pentecostal Church. He held the position of secretary-treasurer for the Wisconsin western section from 1957 to 1964.

In the fall of 1957 while he was still working at the rubber company and assisting Brother Davis, my father's feet and legs developed a strange numbness, and he began to fall. The following spring he was diagnosed as having multiple sclerosis, which ultimately causes paralysis. By fall he could no longer work and was paralyzed from his waist down. By April 1961 my fifty-six-year-old father was confined to a wheelchair. At fifty-two his wife Helen learned to drive and found a job at a health-care facility.

I returned from Apostolic Bible Institute in 1961 shocked to see my previously active father in a wheelchair. The fire of the Holy Ghost comforted him and he said, "The Lord has given me contentment." He loved to play his guitar, sing, worship with visitors, and write poetry.

For thirty years my mother tenderly cared for my father. His last years were very painful, and the last seven months he required twenty-four hour care in a health-care facility. On September 10, 1987, he went to be with the Lord.

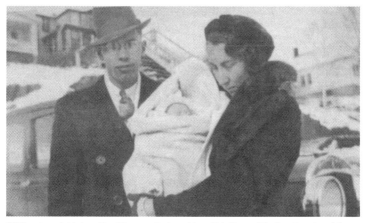

Clifford and Helen Haskins and daughter, Wyllis, with the trusty old car that carried them to Spooner, Wisconsin, each Sunday, 1936.

Dedication of Pentecostal Assembly Stone Church, July 3, 1949, Bro. Haskins leading with visiting ministry in background.

Bro. Haskins still able to sing with his daughter, Wyllis Peuse, at home in Eau Claire, Wisconsin 1984.

10

JAMES H. HASSELL

by Betty Jo Farrar

Before my father and mother took their first church in Gasconade, Missouri, we lived in St. Louis and attended Brother Hite's church.

When the Lord told my folks to go to Gasconade, Dad agreed to go if He would provide. They went to the train station, and as they stood there, someone came up and said, "God told me to give you your train fare."

When I was three, Dad began to pastor at Gasconade. As Mom and Dad prayed that God would supply their needs, a family in town who owned a grocery store came with groceries.

We lived close to a railroad, and hobos soon learned where to come for food. Mom fixed a table and chairs on the back porch especially for them. One day as she saw a tramp coming through the gate, however, she felt God say, "Don't let this man in." She called us children, locked the door, and whispered, "Keep quiet!" Doris and I hid under the bed as Mom kept the baby Edith quiet. The man knocked and called, "Let me in! I know you are in there!" Finally he went away angry, but God kept His protective hand over us.

We moved to Evansville, Indiana, when I was five. Some church folks let us live in a one-room building. With a bed, stove, table and chairs, and baby bed, it looked like a playhouse, but we called it home. We lived there for about a year and a half. During that time, Dad preached at Boonville, Indiana, and other churches nearby. We always went to church no matter where we lived or whether we had proper clothing.

Then Dad pastored the Upper Hills Union Church thirty miles from Evansville near Griffin. My husband, Harold Farrar, now pastors there.

People from denominational churches for miles around, even from Kentucky and Illinois thirty to forty miles away, came to hear the new preacher. The all-day meetings with singing and dinner on the ground are still talked about.

Dad received three to four dollars a week for pastoring the church, but some people donated home-canned fruit, meat, and chickens. Mother often said, "Children, we don't have much to eat but let's pray." Soon someone came bringing food.

Everyone enjoyed the days when the ladies made chowder and chicken and dumplings to be sold by the quart. Members as well as others donated food from their large gardens.

Daddy had an old Model T Ford dedicated to the Lord's work. By the time we got to Sunday school, both running boards were full, two or three people sat on the hood, and we sat two or three deep inside.

Grandma and Grandpa Hassell lived in St. Louis when we lived at Upper Hills, so we always tried to go there for Christmas. Sometimes the flood waters came. If the car drowned, we would just sit and sing songs about the Lord, waiting and praying for the car to start. Many times we got stuck in the dirt and gravel leading to the old black-top highway. When those flood waters came, older ones carried little ones to the car parked on higher ground. When church time came, we went!

Once we had a flat tire on a hill. Basil Fetcher hopped out with the rest of us and started putting the car up on the jack. Mother stood in front of the car when suddenly the jack fell off. She fell but Basil shoved her out of the way of the rolling car.

We liked country living. Dad especially liked the hog butcherings, and we all liked the fresh pork meat. Wheat-threshing time excited us despite all the hard work. The neighbors and friends were like one big happy family. Even the sinners came to Sunday school and church.

Since I was the oldest, Dad took me with him to visit the sick. Mom worked hard and didn't have much time to go. She washed on a rubboard, which meant hard work during long revivals as she washed for the evangelist also.

Mother didn't have many dresses, but I complained about not having "clothes like the other kids." Mama explained, "Honey, look at me. I don't have nice things either." "Well," I said selfishly, "People don't look at you like they do me. You don't need but two or three dresses." Clothes never kept Mom away from church.

When my baby brother Richard was born, he took whooping cough while Mom was still in bed. We almost lost him, but the Lord came to the rescue.

One night after leaving church, someone said, "Look how the sky is lit up!" "Look's like a fire," Dad said, driving fast. A mile from home as we topped the levee, we saw our house burning. We stood there crying as it burned to the ground. Dad had worked at an assessment job for the county along with other jobs besides preaching, so he had some money. He had bought Mom a new Maytag washing machine, had bought everyone a new coat and had stocked up on canned goods and groceries. We lost everything in that fire.

The John Guller family took us home with them. Later we moved to the Maier farm. With the help of the church and the community, Mom and Dad started over again.

Jeannette was born while we lived at the Maier farm. I dressed my blue-eyed baby sister prettily and combed her blond curls. I loved that job!

Seven years later the doctor told Mom, "Twins." Dad said, "Oh, no!" but it was, "Oh, yes!"

When I was in the sixth grade, Dad gave up the church, taking a job in Evansville. Then we moved to St. Louis, where the twins, Brenda Lou and Carolyn Sue, were born six weeks premature. Dad worked in an upholstering shop, but the twins have been a blessing to my parents, keeping them young.

I married, and seventeen months after the twins were born, I presented Mother and Dad with a grandson. Before long grandchildren were playing with the twins.

My parents moved around some before Dad pastored another church, but he preached wherever he had the opportunity. Sometimes preachers get discouraged when they have a family to support. But my daddy knew the power of God and His calling in his life. It was like fire shut up in his bones. When the twins were in the seventh grade, the folks took the church at Cambria, Illinois, and the twins helped them. They finished high school and married before Mother and Dad left to take the McClure, Illinois, church.

Dad always said, "I'm not giving up preaching, just slowing down." He didn't think he would accept another church, but the Buckner church wouldn't take no for an answer. My parents enjoyed being there very much. The people were wonderful, but Dad had a heart attack and was unable to continue. They bought a small home in Tamaroa, Illinois. After another bad attack, Dad had a pacemaker put in.

While lingering between life and death, Dad had a beautiful vision of heaven. The gate opened partly and he saw angels around it, but they told him he could not go in yet. Like Hezekiah of old, Dad asked God to spare him. That has been over seven years ago. The doctor told him not to exert his body by preaching, but he does what he is called upon to do as God gives him strength.

The folks now make their home church at Duquoin, Illinois, where Brother McKinnies pastors. He takes care of them like family, which means so much to us children.

For their fifty-eighth anniversary, the Duquoin church had a reception for Mom and Dad. They invited all the family and many ministers from other churches. They went all out with a photographer, lots of food, and even a skit. What a precious memory for all of us!

Before long, Mom and Dad will celebrate their sixty-sixth anniversary. They have had many hardships and sufferings, but God has blessed abundantly. His grace has been sufficient for them.

Rev. and Mrs. James H. Hassell and Becky Jo, 1928.

Rev. and Mrs. James Hassell, 1970.

Rev. and Mrs. James Hassell and family.

Dedication service at the Hassells' first pastorate in a community church building in Gasconade, Missouri, 1928-30.

11

GUY R. HOMES

from the July, 1976 Voice of Pentecost
William Turner, Editor

The July 1976 issue of the Arizona district paper car-
ried an article about Arizona's Apostolic pioneers. The
paper recapped the story of the outbreak of the Pentecostal
movement beginning in Topeka, Kansas, about the turn of
the century. The revival spread across the nation to
Houston, Texas, to Azusa Street in Los Angeles, back to the
Midwest, to the East, and around the world. The article
included remarks about a number of significant leaders.

One such man was Guy R. Homes, Sr., a young Wisconsin minister who sometime before 1914 had received
the Holy Ghost and soon afterward faced opposition from
his own family for his stand on the oneness of the Godhead. Like so many others of his time, the fire of revelation was burning too brightly for him to sit still. With his
brother and their families, Brother Homes headed west,
at first for Texas, where jobs would support a missionary
work. But God had other plans. It soon became clear to
him that the Lord intended for him to move on, so that in
the year 1914, the first known Oneness Pentecostal
preacher arrived in Arizona.

Guy R. Homes settled his family in Phoenix, a logical choice as the capital had a central location in the state. A carpenter by trade, Homes secured work and a home for his family. He located on the west side of the city, near the state fairgrounds, then on the edge of town.

Phoenix presented a strange environment to the Homeses. It had hot, dusty summers but no modern inventions of evaporative coolers or air conditioners.

For a home Brother Homes found an old wood frame store with living quarters in the back. It faced Grand Avenue and the irrigation canal, near the intersection of Grand Avenue and McDowell Road, only a brief walk from the streetcar stop at six points. Orange groves and canal systems crisscrossed the urban area. A hallway separated the living area from the adjoining rooms of another family. Their mission chapel met in the storefront.

Prayer preceded every major step in the lives of the Homeses. They took their mission seriously; it represented an outpost for truth. So Brother and Sister Homes entered their new quarters in fervent prayer and rebuked the devil from room to room as they settled in.

For the next ten years or so, Brother Homes remained practically the only voice for truth in Arizona. (Another pioneer in the 1920s was a Brother Connelly. Unfortunately, little could be learned of his ministry. He apparently arrived some years after Brother Homes.)

Brother Homes and his brother soon parted over the question of the Godhead—Brother Homes standing firmly for the one God message, his brother and others in the family holding to a doctrine of two persons in the Godhead. The "two God" movement, in fact, flourished through the late 1920s in the Phoenix area.

The mission work on Grand Avenue continued on. In the summertime services were held outside on the lawn. A horse trough served as a baptismal tank. Slowly but steadily the work of God began to grow.

Brother Homes had helpers, particularly in later years, but one of his chief supporters was a daughter, Virginia. She would later become the wife of Brother G. E. Wesson, superintendent of the Arizona District of the United Pentecostal Church for many years.

By the mid thirties other Oneness outposts were established in the Phoenix area. One was known as the Sawdust Mission on East Washington. Later on, others came, such as Alice Sheets and her husband, who before and after their work in Phoenix at a location known as the Sunshine Mission carried the gospel as missionaries to China.

After years of standing alone, the chance for fellowship was precious to the Homeses. When they could, they and those who worked with them gave a helping hand to the other outposts of truth.

By the 1930s Brother Homes had carved out a small church that held on determinedly to the Apostles' doctrine, and his unswerving loyalty to the truth became a lighthouse for others. In those days no organized fellowship had emerged in Arizona, and not every mission work had such strong leadership. Brother Homes himself had to rely on the gift of discernment at times to know when a false prophet had come to town. On more than one occasion a traveling evangelist would come by with a declaration that he was sent by God to minister to them. Sometimes it was so. Sometimes it was not.

At the Sawdust Mission, the situation had gotten out

of hand. Temporarily without a qualified pastor, the little mission had allowed an evangelist to preach for them who soon began to espouse the trinitarian position on the Godhead. Further, the man had fallen into the error of snake handlers—those who "proved their faith" by handling poisonous snakes during church services.

The snake-handling evangelist soon had the people under his control and was drawing large crowds. He then began to mock those who preached baptism in Jesus' name and the oneness of the Godhead, declaring that if God were truly with the Oneness people, then someone from their ranks would have the faith to handle a deadly snake. One of the sisters in the church who was not fooled traveled across town one day to the Grand Avenue Mission in search of help. Working with Brother Homes at the time was Brother Peter Shebley, about twenty-one years old, newly married and zealous for the truth. The woman came to him, explained the situation, and asked for help.

Thinking that truth would not stand such reproach, the young man agreed to come. From then until the next service Brother and Sister Shebley fasted and prayed. He did not believe in snake-handling, but he was determined that if it were necessary, he would do even that to dispel the influence and break the teeth of the "grievous wolf" who had come in among the flock of God.

The night of the service, he took a front-row seat. To his relief, the wooden box in which the rattlesnakes were normally kept was not in its usual position in front of the pulpit. He looked around the platform but the box was gone.

When the service was turned to the snake handler, he

seemed befuddled. "There's been a conspiracy," he declared. "There's not a snake to be found in that whole desert. Something's gone wrong." Suddenly the crowd turned against him, perhaps assuming that he had grown fearful and lacked the faith to produce a snake.

Brother Shebley saw his opportunity. He rose to his feet and declared the whole show had been an ungodly sham. His words struck home, and for the rest of the service, the young man of God was the undisputed master of the situation. He did not dismiss the crowd but he preached. The message was the mighty God in Christ, repentance, baptism in Jesus' name, the infilling of the Holy Ghost, holiness, the whole counsel of God. The enemy had been defeated because a young pioneer had dared to defend the gospel.

Such incidents led godly men to the realization that organized fellowship was needed as a bulwark against false doctrine. Out of that conviction later would emerge the United Pentecostal Church International, its ministers bound willingly to a high standard of ministerial ethics and an unswerving commitment to the fundamental doctrines of the church.

Even without the snake handlers, Pentecost in those days was hardly accepted in the upper levels of society. Speaking in tongues was not the fashionable phenomenon that it is today, and opposition, although not often physical, was everywhere present in the form of false accusations and verbal abuse. On one occasion, young Virginia Homes walked home in tears after a schoolmate accused the Pentecostals of drinking blood in their services. Others held that preachers had some kind of magical powders in their handkerchiefs. All the mopping of the brow while preaching was merely a diversionary tactic for scattering those powders on the people to make them act so strangely. Across town, opposition was continual for one work in east Phoenix during some years of the 1930s. Vandalism, rock throwing, and other interruptions during services were a constant occurrence. And yet, souls were hungry and God was moving.

Brother Homes had a Sunday school. Phillip Diller, uncle of North Phoenix pastor Clyde Diller, served as Sunday school superintendent. The youngsters at about primary age were in the "card class." Their lesson verse was written on the side of a four-by-five card with a picture depicting the lesson scene on the other side. All the classes were held in one room, quite a challenge for students and teachers.

Through the years, Grand Avenue Mission never grew to be very large, but the work remained, staying open when other efforts in later years did not always enjoy such staying power. In 1935, Brother Homes left the Phoenix area and took his family to Atlanta, Georgia, working in a church established by T. C. Montgomery.

In 1938, the burden for the Arizona work once again called him and the family returned. But within a few years, age and hard work took its toll. In 1946, Brother Homes ended his long and faithful pioneer ministry in Arizona. When Brother Homes left for retirement in California that year, Phoenix's population had more than doubled to over 70,000 people since his arrival in 1922. Now other men were coming to take up the torch. A new era was beginning.

The Guy R. Homeses' wedding picture, 1912.

Pastor Guy Ray Homes, Grand Avenue mission.

Pastor Guy R. Homes and congregation in early 1940s.

The Homes family, two sons-in-law, one daughter-in-law and four grand-children.

122

12

PAUL EUGENE HOSCH

by Paul Eugene Hosch

I was born November 10, 1915, in Navarro County, Texas, and have always lived in the great Lone Star State. My father, Lonnie Stinson Hosch, was born in Faulkner, Mississippi, on April 23, 1871. My mother, Frances Melinda Rutherford, was born in the same place on June 8, 1878. Papa's mother died when he was three and his father died when he was eleven. Papa lived with his older brother.

In 1886 when he was fifteen, they moved to Texas. Papa was small for his age, so his brother bought him a half-fare ticket on the train. "Now, Lonnie, when the conductor comes through, look as small as you can," his brother said. So he crouched down and tried to be as little as possible.

My parents met and married in September of 1894. Then along came Loise, Luther, Roy, Lonnie, Nick, Sara Jewell Frances (the first girl was named after her mother and both grandmothers), Otis, Cullen, Allie Mae, and finally a boy named Paul Eugene was number ten. When Papa saw me, he said, "Fannie, if that's the best we can do, we'll quit!"

My parents were Methodists, then Holiness Methodists, then Trinity Methodists until my nineteen-year-old brother, L. J. Hosch, found Acts 2:38 and refused to be baptized in the titles. Later L. J. baptized Papa and Mama and all of us.

I felt that God had called me to preach when I was only four, but I said no to God for ten years. Finally I surrendered on June 6, 1929, at 11:30 p.m. I received the Holy Ghost.

Soon I started teaching young people, and I began preaching some when I was fifteen. When R. L. Blankenship, chairman of the Pentecostal Assemblies of Jesus Christ, visited our church in Gladewater and heard me preach to the young people's group, he wanted to ordain me and send me to South Texas to pastor a church. I told him, "I'm not even a preacher." He said, "Well, whatever you were doing to those young people, they were blessed." I told him that it was just a Bible talk as I was still trying not to preach.

I had seen my brother L. J. suffer so much as a Pentecostal preacher. In those days there were not many tithers, not much organization, and only a few organized churches. Many thought organization was the mark of the beast. I saw L. J. put cardboard in his worn-out shoes. I decided I was not going to be a preacher. I would be a young people's leader, teach Sunday school, play my guitar, sing solos or be in a quartet, pay my tithes and give good offerings out of my $10.50 a week salary but, "Don't ask me to be a preacher!"

I married Doris Voncile Hogg on June 30, 1936. Our first child, Paula, was born October 3, 1937, and a second daughter, ThomasAnn, was born January 21, 1941. By this time I was in charge of the church, but I still said, "I'm not a preacher." I was a board member, secretary-treasurer, Sunday school teacher, young people's leader, and also doing most of the preaching. When World War II came, I traveled around to work in defense plants. I always found a church and assisted the pastor—Dumas, Nederland, Beaumont, and Orange, Texas. In Orange Pastor H. L. Stevens appointed me as Sunday school superintendent. We stayed in Orange for eighteen months, and Brother Stevens said I preached more in the last twelve months than he did.

While I was working in Orange in a shipyard for Consolidated Steel, I consented to God to be a preacher and gave the remainder of my life to work for Him. The Lord had taken all my joy, anointing, and blessing away. Before when I had testified, it blessed all the church. But now when I tried to testify and preach, the anointing was not there. I repented—still no joy. I had a month of that, then I could stand it no longer.

One day at work, painting in the engine room of a destroyer escort ship with Hortman Milner as my partner, I began crying and praying. God said, "The gifts and calling of God are without repentance. If you will obey Me and preach My gospel, I will restore your blessing." I spoke out loud, "It's a deal, I'll do it." Red (as we called Hortman) asked, "What did you say, Preacher? Who were you talking to anyway? You have such a look of relief on your face." I told Red, "I have just given the rest of my life to the Lord to be a full-time preacher."

I stacked my tools and started up the ladder, then thought, I'm supposed to give two weeks' notice to leave the shipyard. I went back to work and as soon as my lead man came around, I told him, "I'll be leaving in two weeks." He warned, "Preacher, you'll be in the army in a month." I replied, "Well, Bud, I'm going to preach two months as a civilian and then begin preaching as a soldier in the army."

God gave me back my blessing and anointing! It was like receiving the Holy Ghost all over again. We moved some of our furniture to my parents and some to Sister Hosch's parents. I went to the district convention and told Elder R. L. Blankenship, "I'm ready to be ordained." I had local license for five years, then was ordained in Milford in 1944.

I asked Brother John E. Dillon of Moss Hill, our sectional elder, to send me where someone needed help. He sent me to Porter, Texas, where the church was split by another group coming in. They got most of the people and the building, leaving the Pentecostal Assemblies of Jesus Christ people without a place to worship. My wife, two daughters, and I arrived there in late 1944 and began to encourage the few who were left. We had the first service in the community building with twelve present.

Before I quit my job, I had planned to go into the furniture business and had $9,754.00 in the bank, a lot of money for me. I purchased one-half acre of land to put a church on, then found an abandoned church building out in the woods and persuaded the owners to give it to us. It cost three hundred dollars to move and block up. We cut new sills out of the pine forest. By this time we had about twenty-five in Sunday school. Eighteen months later our average was sixty-two.

At this time, Sister Hosch had asthma, so we had to move to a higher altitude. But where to go? L. J. Hosch was elected district superintendent at Milford at the convention when I was ordained, and he told me, "There's a small church in Dallas that needs a pastor."

"That town's too big for me. I'm not interested."

"Will you just go up and preach Wednesday night?" he asked.

I agreed but told him again, "I'm not interested in pastoring there."

We went to Dallas in June of 1946. My wife and I sang and I preached "Time Marches On." L. J. met with the board after church. One member insisted that he had seen me in a vision and I was the man. Another said he knew me as a young man and if I would be as good a pastor as I had been as a young man, then I would be a good one. So the board voted one hundred percent for me. L. J. told me about the board vote but I still said, "I'm not interested. Let's go home." He went back to the board but they asked us, "Come back next night and preach again." I agreed.

All day Thursday, we had no food, no fun. I spent all day in the woods in my car praying! Finally I told God, "If You want me there, I'll go if the vote is one hundred percent for me." That night I preached, "Looking unto Jesus" and the board voted one hundred percent for me. Then the church membership voted.

L. J. said, "Son, it's one hundred percent." I asked to count the votes. There were twenty-six. "No, it's not one hundred percent," I insisted. "There are twenty-seven present." Sister Scott, an elderly lady said, "Young man, this is the first time I've been in this church in six months. I did not think I should vote, but if you will be pastor, I'll come all the time." That made one hundred percent.

We moved into the Sunday school rooms at Dallas on July 5, 1946. We started with twenty-seven. The tithes were $17.50 to $50.00 per week, more of the first than the last. I still had some money, however; I transferred $347.00 from Porter to Dallas. I had one wife, two daughters, and one jersey cow named Nellie Bligh. In six months the Sunday school averaged 60 to 75, in twelve months about 110 to 125.

Then it began. The largest family we had, the Laynes, transferred to California. After this 63 people moved away in three weeks. It was not a split; they just left Dallas for various states and different reasons. The next Sunday I took my text from John 6: "Will ye also go away?" but they didn't. So twelve months later we gained from 27 to about 45. We kept on going, and a year later we were back to 125 with a high attendance of 250 later. The finances were about $200.00 per week so all was well.

We had miracles of healing: cancer cured, blind eyes opened, and broken bones instantly healed. The Sunday school grew and in 1954 we sold the property for $12,775.00 and moved to the present location. I resigned July 1, 1980, after thirty-four years as pastor of Emmanuel Pentecostal Church with the church debt free.

Brother Richard W. Flowers was elected pastor on the nominating ballot. The church purchased property on the loop around Dallas, a tremendous location and plan to move.

Let me relate some funny or unusual things that happened while I was pastor. One night we were invited to supper. We ate, visited, and came home about midnight, tired. I put on my short pajamas and was in bed at 12:30. The phone rang. It was my "bachelor boy," my fifty seven-year-old son in the gospel, W. G. He kept all his plans to himself. I wondered why he built a nice three-bedroom brick home, furnished to please any woman. He said, "My, my pastor, where have you been? I've been looking for you for six hours!" I said, "I'm sorry. What's wrong?" He answered, "This is the worst night I have ever had. Come over here quick. I want to get married to Winnie." I told him, "Okay, just let me get dressed." He insisted, "Oh, no, I'm in a hurry. Just come as you are." Well, I read the wedding ceremony, but I did change to my suit and tie.

Another time the phone rang at 4:00 A.M. "I have a pistol pointed at my right temple and I'm gonna kill myself," the man said. I replied, "Well, do you need me to help you?" But he answered, "You're not gonna stop me." I said, "Well, it sounds like you've got your mind made up. I'll just listen." He didn't do it. I never did hear the gun. I was a young pastor then; now I might go over and perhaps he'd shoot both of us.

Once I was in my study on my knees, with my hand over my face bowing over a small daybed. I saw a large hole in the ground. I asked, "God, what does this mean?" Then out of the hole came a casket. Standing up in the casket was Charlie K_____. "God what else?" I asked. The casket and Charlie went back into the hole, then a sign with the figure 2 on it. "Now what, Lord?" The sign went back in the ground then reappeared with the words "two months." So I knew Charlie had two months to get ready.

I had tried for twenty years to get him to come to church with his wife. God had healed him twice when we prayed—a badly broken kneecap that the doctor could not fix and a severe heart attack that the doctor had given up on. But when church was mentioned Charlie always laughed at me. After five days I got his wife to tell him about my vision. The next day he bought a two-thousand-dollar insurance policy.

Sixty days from the day he learned of the vision, he had a stroke in one side but could still talk. He sent for me two days later but I could not have faith this time for him. I tried to talk with him about his soul, but he turned his face away and closed his eyes. The next night he had a stroke in the other side and died seventy days from the vision. He had five extra days to get the message to him and five days of God's mercy. I wondered what else I could have done.

I was in Portland, Oregon, at the general conference of the United Pentecostal Church when I saw a vision of an eighteen-wheeled truck about to run over my daughter in Dallas on the Houston Street viaduct. I prayed. She changed lanes to her left. The truck came on and ripped off the right rear fender of my new '69 VW. I called home and got the story immediately. Then I told my daughter, "Call the insurance company." God has kept His hand upon us and I am grateful!

Editor's note: After Paul E. Hosch wrote this unique story, his wife died on August 4, 1987, and then he went to be with the Lord on June 24, 1988.

Rev. and Mrs. Paul Hosch

"Some are gone but we're still family."

"Let's celebrate!" The Paul Hosches.

13

PAUL H. KLOEPPER

by R. P. Kloepper

On a farm in the territory of Oklahoma about 1906, little Paul prayed his first sincere prayer as he picked up the limp form of his six-year-old brother, Oscar. A mule had kicked his brother unconscious, and ten-year-old Paul felt his need of divine intervention. The answer came.

This first contact with his God, plus others, led Paul Kloepper to a born-again experience at age thirty-two. His active ministry started the next year, 1930, and continued over half a century. As a minister he first joined the Pentecostal Assemblies of the World, then the Pentecostal Assemblies of Jesus Christ, and finally became a charter member of the United Pentecostal Church.

On November 21, 1896, in a farm home near Baldwin, Illinois, Paul was born into a growing family that eventually included seven brothers and two sisters: Edward, Henry, Walter, Ernest, Oscar, Elsie, Ella, Arthur, and Ted. Grandpa Henry Kloepper, along with Grandma Emilie (nee Rinkle), were staunch Lutherans, so after only one year of public school Paul enrolled in a Lutheran Christian school. The pastor was also the teacher. This schooling concluded with confirmation (the time of first communion), and then followed another year of public school.

In 1900 Oklahoma was one of the few territories left. Evidently Grandpa heard of the farm opportunities, so he placed his wife and children on a passenger train while he rode the freight car he had reserved for the household furnishings at one end and the cattle and horses at the other. They settled down near Apache, and Oklahoma was admitted to the United States while they lived there. The Kloeppers became involved in the local Lutheran church after arriving. Farm families helped them adjust; however, after three years, Grandpa moved his family back to southern Illinois, where he farmed until his death four years later.

The traumatic event in Dad's life that caused him to pray occurred while in Oklahoma. He often spoke of being the only one in the room when Grandpa left this world—another event that touched him very deeply.

He assumed responsibility at the farm, then became a hired hand for other farmers. He spent long hours working hard for low pay, so he turned to a developing industry in his area—coal mining. But he did not change before another important event took place that lasted almost sixty-eight years.

At a dance in 1917 this farm boy met a farm girl. A courtship resulted that lasted for fifteen months and ended in a country wedding near Lively Grove, Illinois, on May 26, 1918, when Anna Lehr, also German, became Mrs. Paul Kloepper.

After farming briefly, the couple moved to Marissa, where they bought their first home and their three children were born—Raymond, 1920; Ilene, 1930; and Ann, 1932.

In the mid-1800s Germans, including my great-grand-parents, emigrated from Germany and settled the Marissa area. My grandparents spoke German in their homes, as did my parents. I spoke German till age four, when the need for communicating with English-speaking playmates became a priority.

Dad registered for the World War I draft but was not called before the war ended on the year of their wedding. The recession that followed the war affected the mining jobs, so they farmed for four years. Since there was no Lutheran church in Marissa, the folks became involved in the Evangelical church. Dad served as the church treasurer. Active—yes, but the hunger in his soul continued.

The sovereign God weaves the threads of life so that we can make our choices to fit into His master plan. Two more events in 1928 added more weaving. Most men receive their call to the ministry after they are born again—not so with my father. He had been up all night with his sick mother, driven some distance, cared for the morning chores at the farm, and then lain down for some much-needed rest.

A vision came forcibly! A ladder stretched from earth to heaven with many people trying to climb it. Some made a few rounds then fell back down. Others climbed further but also failed to reach heaven. Some did reach the top, but found that right in front of heaven's door, Satan stood still trying to win the victory over their lives. Then the Lord asked my father to help these people who were trying to make heaven their home. For about a year the vision could not be applied to Paul's life.

The second event in Paul's life that year was a visit to the Price healing campaign in Belleville. Mother was not

135

well, so they went for prayer. She was not healed, but when Elder John 0. Underwood, the local Pentecostal pastor, dismissed the service that night, his prayer touched my father so deeply that he said, "I must find that man's church!"

The following year Dad's Uncle Bill Rinkle visited, and the healing campaign and Brother Underwood were mentioned. Uncle Bill knew where the church was located and took my folks there. A little later Mother was healed at another Pentecostal revival in our home town, where her cousin, Dorothy Elser, was the evangelist. Both Mom and Dad were baptized in Jesus' name at Belleville and filled with the Holy Ghost with the evidence of speaking with tongues.

During repentance Dad tried to break his habit of chewing tobacco. One morning he threw it away, but it hit a peach tree and fell to the ground. Satan said, "You know where it is when you need it." Dad picked it up and threw it over the fence—never to touch tobacco again.

Mother received the Spirit first on a Thursday night. About 2:30 A.M. Friday she heard a noise and thought, An intruder is in the house. It was my dad, seeking the new experience. The following Sunday, the Lord told Dad to fast for the first time in his life and he would receive the Holy Ghost that night. Fast he did and the baptism came within a few minutes at the altar.

Dad became an avid Bible reader, beginning his ministry the next year. We had no air conditioning or electric fans, so during the heat he lay on the cooler linoleum floor with his Bible in his hands studying for hours. "Praise the Lord" or "Oh, thank you, Lord" punctuated his conversation wherever he was. His meditation, study, and prayer brought the anointing upon his ministry. His jovial smile, quick wit, stoicism, and punctuality enhanced his ministry. His earlier shyness became a "holy boldness" in the pulpit.

To many, 1929 means the economic crash and the beginning of the Great Depression. Although it affected my family economically, yet 1929 brings memories of a new birth, a new life, and a great spiritual awakening in our homes.

Parents do affect their children. At that time I was the only child, and I noticed that we went to church a lot more—twice on Sunday with cottage meetings through the week. Two neighboring farm families came to the Lord at the same time: the Bald family and the Stehl family, my Uncle Henry, Aunt Mary, and Cousin Irene. These spiritually hungry families met almost nightly for prayer after working hard, long days in the wheat harvest. Although they prayed until midnight, 4:00 A.M found them up ready for another day.

The winds of Pentecost brought other changes. Dad didn't chew tobacco anymore; there was no more social drinking, no more cursing, but much talk of "going to heaven." About three weeks after my folks received their personal Pentecost, I came to Mother with tears streaming down my face and said, "I want to go to heaven, too!" In less than a month, as an eight-year-old boy I also received the Holy Ghost.

Elder J. O. Underwood of Belleville, Illinois, was our first pastor. Many ministers came from this assembly: M. J. Wolff, Jim Gardner, Paul Froese, Carl Froese, Carl Harris, Lester Harris, my father, and others. A second generation of ministers has come from this Belleville group. Our next home church was Marissa, pastored by Frank Barton, Lloyd Calvert, and J. O. McCoin. My sisters, Ilene and Ann, born a few years later, were touched by parental influence and received their Pentecost while still quite young.

Although Dad did not get to develop his keen mind further in a higher institution of learning, he and Mother sacrificed to educate their children. Ilene, Ann, and I all graduated with teaching degrees from Southern Illinois University at Carbondale, for which we are grateful to our parents.

In the early 1930s Dad ministered in various churches with his first regular ministry in his home town of Baldwin in 1932-33. He preached revivals in Illinois, Missouri, Kentucky, and Indiana. He pastored at McKinley Station, Illinois, from 1935 to 1938—a rural church near Coulterville.

Mom supported his ministry by ministering to the sick and needy. Every visitor to our home left with a gift—a loaf of bread, a jar of chili sauce, a coffee cake, or a slip from a plant produced by her green thumb. She taught Sunday school and worked with the ladies of the various churches, never complaining of the changes in pastorates.

After ministering at Glendale from 1941 to 1942, the folks moved to Murphysboro. Later they pastored at Logan Hollow near Cora from 1944 to 1953. Here a young Bible school graduate, Calvin Rigdon, preached one of his earlier revivals and became a lifelong family friend. Here Sisters Charlotte and Nilah also came for special meetings.

Another ten-year pastorate followed at Grayville from 1954 to 1964. Then Dad thought he would retire, and they moved back to Marissa to the house where their children were born.

Sparta was only ten miles away, and the next year the church there needed a pastor. At almost sixty-nine, Dad didn't give it much thought at first, then the Lord spoke to him, "What are you going to do about Sparta? You are called to go to Sparta." Here Sister Betty Kloepper and I did some of our home missions work for the three years Dad was there.

Dad's ministry did not stop with a second retirement. They sold their home in Marissa and moved to Grayville, where he served as interim pastor, preached special meetings, taught the Bible class very capably, and conducted funerals.

Finally, at eighty-five Dad chose not to renew his driver's license, which immobilized him in the next few years. The Kloepper family grew from two to twenty-four including six grandchildren—Raymond II, Claudette, Steven, Janet, Sherrie, and Scott—and five great-grandchildren. In his ninetieth year Paul Kloepper had lived to be the oldest of approximately four hundred ministers of the Illinois District of the United Pentecostal Church International. He cherished so much the plaque that is given to U.P.C.I. ministers with fifty years or more of service.

A complication of illnesses required his residence in the Skilled Care Unit of Carmi Township Hospital for the last nine months of his life. Mother was his roommate, and their friends and relatives could visit with them. The final goodbye was March 25, 1986.

The testimonies at the memorial service serve to reveal Dad's personality. When Kenneth Reeves was seventeen, he held his third revival for my father and stayed in my parents' home. While there Brother Reeves became very ill with the flu. "They cared for me as if I were their own," he recalled. Through the years Brother Reeves has told me of Dad's counsel during that visit. He advised, "Don't get too self-righteous and be too hard on the people when they make mistakes. People need mercy. The harder you are on people, you'll find that you will face the same test yourself, and you might fail also. People who fail need a friend. Have a forgiving spirit and try to help those who have failed. Don't be too harsh." Brother Reeves feels that his book *Justice with Mercy* had some of its roots in that early counsel with my dear dad.

By her own request Dad's granddaughter Claudette gave a beautiful tribute. The heritage of truth that has now passed through four generations meant more to her than any other inheritance. C. L. McKinnies represented the Illinois District to honor the oldest of its ministers. Edward Lucas brought comfort from his text in Job.

Dad's ministry has not ceased. It is being carried on by four ministers in the family: a son, R. P. Kloepper; a grandson, Scott Graham; two grandsons-in-law, Marvin Walker and Eddie Cupples. Another grandson, Dr. R. P. Kloepper II, a deacon and active layman, also carries the message inherited from his grandfather. That Good Friday afternoon, with the sun shining across the sloping hillside, was not an end but merely the changing of the guard.

Rev. and Mrs. Paul H. Kloepper, 1976.

Newlyweds, Paul H. Kloepper and Anna Lehr Kloepper.

Paul H. Kloepper

Bro. Kloepper preaches the Word in the early 1940s.

"Giddyap! Let's go!" 1917.

143

Oscar Edward Lamb and family. Left to right: Rhonda Click, Teresa Bowen, David Lamb, Ruth Cockran, Martha McDuffie, James E. Lamb, Mary Cheatham, Barbara Whitehead, Walter Halbert Lamb, Shirley Fischer, Edna Nation, Katie Lamb, Oscar Edward Lamb. (Saundra Eckstadt was not present.)

14

OSCAR EDWARD LAMB

by Edna Nation

On October 1, 1915, Oscar Edward Lamb was born. "My first son," smiled Annie to her husband, Ed. "Don't you think he's a fine looking boy?"

"He looks like a fine fellow to me," responded her husband. "Here! Let me take a good look at him. Yes, he's one fine fellow." The proud parents were E. D. and Annie Barrentine Lamb of Attala County, Mississippi. O. E. was to be the third of twelve children, the first of eight sons. "The Lambs always have many sons," said Annie, "but it'll take one strappling of a boy to beat this one!"

Oscar Edward Lamb had the advantage of early childhood training. He was born into a Christian home; he was taught right from wrong, about repentance and restitution, and many other things. "Even though my mother never actually joined the Church of God, she was loosely affiliated with it," explained O. E. "They believed in and taught holiness. They also believed in the trinity, which meant they believed in three separate and distinct persons in the Godhead. Mother taught her children about God, and when she went to church, it was to the Church of God. And so she said we were Church of God."

O. E. didn't join any church. Once when he attended his mother's church, somebody tried to get him to go to the mourner's bench, shake the preacher's hand, be saved, and become a member of the church. He replied, "Oh, no! You won't be getting me to do that!" The person talking to him asked, "Why not?" "'Cause shaking the preacher's hand won't get you anywhere, fellow! Don't you know that? I don't know much about the Bible, but I have read enough to know better than that!" declared the twelve-year-old Oscar Lamb, and so he stubbornly refused to join the church, even though most of his friends were joining.

He asked them, "How long do you think this religion you just got is gonna last?"

"I don't know. Why?" someone asked.

"Well, I know!" Oscar chuckled. "It won't last long. The reason's 'cause you didn't get any power with it. Just you wait till the first temptation comes along—you'll be falling right back out there in sin. When you really get religion, it gets in you, and it changes you! And until I get the life-changing kind, I won't be getting any! And wait until summer is over. You'll be right back out there in the world with the rest of us, having fun! Just you wait and see!" And so he continued his frolicking and fun, for O. E. Lamb loved having a good time.

When the leaves began turning in the fall and the harvest was over, the younger set began having dances. "Come on!" they called. Without hesitation, the new church members joined the rest of the crowd, and they danced all night long.

"Our favorite pastime was dancing," declared O. E.

"This was the way we handled it. We decided whose house we'd meet at. Then we'd go into the parlor, stack all the parlor furniture against the wall, and use the open floor for dancing. One night we danced so long, the floor caved in." O. E. chuckled at the memory, then continued, "I don't remember what happened next. I just remember we were all in trouble over that floor."

During the summer of 1935, Zachary Spears conducted revival services in Attala County, Mississippi. While there, he stayed in the home of Josh and Delza Ellard, and services were held in the Ellards' parlor. Zachary Spears, an old-time preacher man, was a One God preacher. He also baptized his candidates by immersion in Jesus' name. Soon Attala County was humming with the news of this new way of baptizing, for no one in the county had preached such a "strange doctrine" before. So the people came, a few at a time, to the Ellards' parlor to listen to Zachary Spears. Some liked what they heard, while others didn't like it at all. Still they came and listened. One of those who came and listened was twenty-year-old Oscar Edward Lamb.

The first time he went to hear the preacher, it was through no desire of his own, but to pay a social debt. One of his former girlfriends pleaded with him to escort her to the service and then back home. "Please," she begged. "I need your protection. I've just gotten word straight that seven boys are planning to waylay me on the road to church tonight, and if you're with me, I know they won't bother me." So Oscar took a girl to church.

"I sat back there, with a girl on both sides, and I couldn't concentrate on the sermon, 'cause they wouldn't leave me alone, but I heard enough. I knew I needed to hear some more preaching like that," declared O. E. "You could tell by the way he preached, the man of God had something that I needed." O. E. paused for reflection, and as he relived the scene, he continued, "Once, during that first sermon, I got called outside, 'cause the leader of the group of boys wanted to whip me. So I went out, gave the boy a good talk, told him if he was looking for trouble he had found it, and then I went back into the service. After that situation was settled, I was better able to hear the rest of the sermon. Those boys never bothered either me or the girl again.

"That night, I met for the first time Josh Ellard, who was first beginning to feel his call to preach; Josh's wife, Delza; Bertha Ellard Cook; and Annie Mae Ellard Townsend. They were the brother and two sisters of Katie Ellard. And of course I saw Katie again, the most beautiful girl I ever saw in my whole life." Lamb paused and reflected, "Of course, I had my eyes on Katie, and her brother, Josh, knew it, so he and I didn't get along so well. But Delza, she was different. She worked with me, 'cause she knew the power of God could change me. Delza saw what God could do for me.

"The first time I saw Katie, I drove an ice truck by her house. When I tried to sell ice to her, she looked up at me with those beautiful blue eyes and said, 'I'm sorry, I don't have any money.' I said, 'That's okay, honey, I'll give you ice anytime you want it.' And so I started stopping and giving her ice, just so I could look at her. She was beautiful!"

O. E. Lamb went to work seriously courting Katie, whom everyone called Donnie. He had a rough time with Bessie Rule Ellard, Donnie's mother, who was protective of her daughter. "The first time I came to see Donnie, her mother wouldn't let me inside the house. I could see a good roaring fire in the fireplace, and it was cold outside, so I appealed to her maternal nature, and she let me in to warm myself, even though her 'Tss . . .' showed her feelings and disapproval. I realized I'd have to go slow with Bessie Ellard, so I stayed only a few minutes, thanked her politely, and left. Right away, I realized, I must win the approval of this lady somehow; otherwise, she'll never give me the hand of her daughter in marriage!" So he set out to make friends with Katie's mother.

The next time Oscar Lamb attended church, he drove his black 1935 Ford sedan. He had finally gotten permission to take the beautiful Katie Leonie Ellard to church in his sedan. Mallie Morgan, Delza's sister, was their chaperone.

The whole way there and back Aunt Mallie talked about the Holy Ghost and how wonderful it was," he recalled. "The way she described it made me so hungry for God. I didn't know what to do. I finally said, 'You're gonna hafta stop talking about it, or I'm gonna hafta stop this car right here and pray, 'cause I want the Holy Ghost so much!' She just laughed and kept talking. We finally made it to church.

That night the preacher preached hellfire and brimstone. He pointed that bony finger straight at me and named every sin I'd been doing. I thought he would never stop preaching so I could pray. The load of sin and guilt was so heavy upon my soul, I thought I could bear it no longer. I whispered, "Lord, if You'll just help that preacher to quit preaching long enough so I can pray, I'll be much obliged to You!" Soon afterwards, the altar appeal was given, and I went to an old-fashioned altar of repentance.

That first night, I prayed for three hours and I felt somewhat better. Most of the heavy load was lifted; however, there was some restitution I had to handle before all my guilt would leave. That night as I prayed, things came before me. I remembered some chickens I had stolen. The Lord let me know I'd have to confront the owner, confess, and pay for those chickens. The next day, I was out and about, making restitution. Now I'm ready to get the Holy Ghost, I decided. I prayed a long time the next night, but still I didn't speak in tongues.

The next evening I said, "I'm going early tonight. I want to get started praying early, 'cause I'm getting down to business tonight! I can't stand it any longer! I must have the Holy Ghost!"

And so Oscar Edward Lamb, who usually dressed fashionably, forgot his pride and pulled on some Big Smith overalls. "I want to be comfortable! I don't want my clothes to hinder me!" he decided.

Church started early, with someone singing about the judgment day and about folks needing to repent and pray. Oscar interrupted the singing. "Please, folks!" he pleaded, "Could you stop that singing? I can't stand it any longer without the Holy Ghost! Could you please pray for me?"

Oscar began praying at three o'clock in the afternoon. His friend, Mr. Carmeans, joined him at the altar. Three hours later, Mr. Carmeans broke through, speaking in tongues as the Spirit of God gave him utterance, but Oscar was still praying. After Mr. Carmeans enjoyed his experience for a while, he began praying with his friend. Four hours passed. Five hours. *I wonder what the problem is?* some thought, but they prayed on. Six hours

150

passed. Some turned away, for they were exhausted, and they knew they had to get some sleep before the next day's labor, but still Oscar earnestly sought God to fill him with His Spirit. "Fill my soul with something that will last me when this old world is on fire," he prayed. He continued to press forward in his prayers, even though his bones ached and he was hurting all over.

Oscar later testified, "At the end of seven long hours of prayer, a bolt of yellow fire came through the ceiling of the room, hit my head with great force, and I was slain in the Spirit. Of course, when the Spirit hit me, I wilted to the floor. Falling flat on my back, I began speaking in other tongues as the Spirit of God gave the utterance. It was wonderful! It was glorious! I lay there, glorifying God, speaking in other tongues. I knew now that God had finally poured out on me something that was worthwhile, something that was lasting, something that would keep me when this world was on fire!

"While I was 'slain,' I knew everything that was going on around me. I was conscious of people praying and worshiping God. I was not out. I was in another world, yes; caught up, yes; powerless to come back until God got finished with me. But I was very aware of everything. I met reality that night. I met God face to face, and He showed me some things. I wouldn't take anything for the experience I received from God that night. And thank God for my friends who prayed with me for the full seven hours! Delza Ellard and my friend Carmeans stayed the full watch.

"On the way home from church that night, Mallie Morgan, Delza's sister, and my friend Carmeans tried to explain baptism in the name of Jesus. It wasn't making any sense to me. Finally, I stopped them and prayed, 'Lord, if what they're saying is true, and there is only one God, please show me, 'cause I can't understand and accept it unless You show me!' As soon as those words tumbled from my mouth, a bright light shone into my car, and it almost blinded me, so that I had to slow the '35 Ford sedan and pull it over to the side, almost stopping, for when the revelation of One God came, baptism in the name of Jesus came also. The blinding yellow light of God's divine power shone brightly as the glorious revelation came to me. After that experience, I could never once doubt it, but had to declare it!

"After I spoke in tongues for one hour, my cup of joy full and running over, I wanted to tell everybody I saw about this experience. Naturally, one of my first thoughts was of my friends, so the next day, I went to see them and told them of my new-found joy in the Holy Ghost. They laughed in my face!"

One of them said, "Oscar Lamb, I'm surprised at you, of all people! I just hadn't put you in the category with those summertime Christians, those who get religion every summer, then backslide during the winter." Then they laughed and declared, "Just you wait till fall comes, you'll be out there with the best of us, dancing till the floors cave in, 'cause you love dancing too much to give it up!"

"Oh, no!" Oscar exclaimed, "I won't be back! You see, I haven't given up dancing; I've just changed partners! You won't see me running with the crowd, dancing all night anymore! I got something real, something wonderful, something that will keep me when this world is on fire!"

Lamb's friends gave him a look of astonishment, scoffed, turned, and walked away, not believing Oscar Lamb would change his lifestyle. They soon found out that he meant every word he said, for God called him to preach, though it took a while for him to accept the call.

"Thank God, I lived to see the day my mother and father received the truth, as did also most of their sons and daughters—all but one, an older sister, who refused to turn her back on the doctrine of the trinity. She remained a member of the Church of God until she was laid to rest. I did my part in bringing this gospel to my family, to my own children, and to many other people through the raising up of works in many places."

In 1939, O. E. Lamb quit a job with the U.S. Corps of Engineers so he could "spend more time studying and preparing for the ministry." In the late '30s and early '40s, he wasted no time hitting the evangelistic trail, pitching the big-top tent and preaching revivals in places like Kennett, Missouri, where his friend Carmeans was from, and then in other towns in Missouri, including Poplar Bluff. He and his family suffered hardships and faced obstacles like rotten tomatoes thrown at the preacher, but they enjoyed victories also. God used O. E. Lamb mightily, giving him power to overcome every temptation, no matter how severe the trial. God came through with miracles of healing, salvation of souls, and lives changed for eternity.

This old-time preacher man started the first church at Pascagoula, Mississippi, at 520 East Lincoln Avenue. The street name has since been changed to Ingalls, commemorating the Ingalls shipbuilding industry in the city. After building and pastoring the First Pentecostal Church of Pascagoula, Mississippi, for seven years the young pastor resigned, installing another pastor to carry on the work.

During his evangelistic tenure, O. E. Lamb conducted cottage prayer meetings or revivals that resulted in the nucleus of churches in such places as Batesville, Locke Station (Marks), Clarksdale, Lambert, Hesterville, and Carmack in Mississippi and Covington in Louisiana.

During the fifty-five years of his ministry, O. E. Lamb witnessed many miracles. Blinded eyes were opened on at least two occasions. Ears became unstopped. He rejoiced to see the crippled leap out of their wheelchairs and walk. He has been touched by the despair of a family as they waited with a loved one who was lying in a coma, seeing, yet unseeing, in a vegetable state. He has rejoiced with them when, at God's bidding, he prayed the prayer of faith and spoke to the comatose individual to be healed and awake from his sleep. Then he saw the man awake and go home with his family. These and many other mighty wonders and miracles of healing has he seen, all done in the mighty and wonderful name of Jesus Christ and for His glory.

O. E. and Katie Lamb are the parents of twelve children: Edna, Shirley, Hal, Barbara, Mary, James Edward, Martha, Ruth, Teresa, David Lamar, Saundra, and Rhonda. Five of the girls married preachers and are endeavoring to carry on the work begun by their father and mother.

To God be the glory forever!

Before the twins, Saundra and Rhonda, were born.

O. E. Lamb, his wife, and young family (Edna, Hal, and Shirley) on the evangelistic trail in southeast Missouri in the early '40s.

Bro. and Sis. Lamb with the twins, Rhonda and Saundra.

Bro. Lamb relaxes.

The Lambs celebrate their golden anniversary with daughter Edna and son-in-law, Ronald Nation.

15

SAMUEL CALVIN MCCLAIN

by Charles McClain

Samuel Calvin McClain was born February 25, 1889, in the state of Georgia to Samuel Bryant McClain and Laura Batchelor McClain. At the early part of this century, Sam C. McClain was among the pioneers who joined the Pentecostal movement. He received the Holy Ghost as a teenage boy while teaching school in central Arkansas and began preaching in 1912. His first converts were members of his own family and some of the young people that he taught in school.

Always seeking all that God had for him, it is not surprising that he was among the first Pentecostals to understand the oneness of the Godhead. And upon this truth he stood firm for the rest of his life.

Sam McClain married Bessie Ann Rodgers in Eureka Springs, Arkansas, on February 23, 1919. They were deeply involved in the work of God together until her death on May 4, 1966.

In those early days revivals were not planned a year in advance. They were planned while he was on his knees seeking God's will and direction for his life. He and his wife, Bessie, an ordained minister herself, lived by faith and were led by the Lord. Aunt Bessie had the faith that could move mountains, and if you were not sincere in your walk with God, you had better get out of her way.

A revival for Uncle Sam and Aunt Bessie would typically start with both of them on their knees before the Lord waiting for instructions. Most times they were told to catch a certain train. Once on the train, God would tell them just where to get off. When they got off the train, they would walk up and down the streets of the strange city until God would show them just which house they were to approach. Since God always does things well, inside that house would be someone who had been praying for God to send someone with the message.

Now the revival could begin. First those of the household would be saved, then the neighbors, and then others in the town. When they would outgrow the house, porch, and yard, a church would have to be built. This is where Uncle Sam would shine. His calling was to break new ground and plant churches.

When the church was well established, the Lord would send a good pastor to take over so Uncle Sam and Aunt Bessie could be free to carry the message to another town. The fruits of their labor can be found all over the Southwest today.

At the beginning of the Pentecostal movement in the early 1900s, there were too few preachers to have much fellowship with each other. At this time there was a Bible school in Eureka Springs, Arkansas, established by a Sister Barnes. It was here that many of the preachers of that time would come for fellowship, to renew their spirits, and to build up their faith.

They would set the table for a meal even when they had no food in the house to cook. They would gather around the table and start praying. Soon they would hear a knock on the door and there would be food for the meal. What a way to learn to use your faith!

At one of these gatherings at the school Uncle Sam had a desperate need. He told the Lord he just had to have a new suit before going back on the field. "My suit is in threads, Lord!" A letter arrived from a dear saint somewhere, and in it was ten dollars for Uncle Sam. After having himself a little shout, he started to town to get that much-needed suit. On the way, God spoke to Uncle Sam and told him to return to the school. "Someone is praying there who needs that ten dollars." Uncle Sam tried to argue with the Lord, but finally he knew he had to yield to the will of God.

Upon returning to the school, he found B. H. Hite on his knees. "Here is the answer to your prayer," Uncle Sam said as he handed Brother Hite the money. Now it was Brother Hite's turn to shout. It seems that God had told Brother Hite to go to St. Louis to start a work, but he needed at least ten dollars to get there.

Uncle Sam always took credit for making my marriage possible. You see, Sister Stella Guinn was one of the first ones saved under Brother Hite's ministry, and my wife, Jane, is Sister Guinn's daughter. God works in mysterious ways!

One of Uncle Sam's passions was to have part in as many new churches as he could. Every time he heard of a new church starting anywhere, he would send an offering. He always said that by helping, even in a small way, he would have a part in every soul that would ever be saved in that church.

As Uncle Sam and Aunt Bessie grew a little too old for traveling, they moved to Tupelo, Mississippi. Uncle Sam taught at the Pentecostal Bible Institute there. He was certainly an inspiration to all the students who sat in his classes. His telling of all the times that God had delivered him instilled a strong faith in all of us. Some leading preachers who learned under him and are still active are E. J. McClintock, E. E. Judd, E. E. Jolley, and George Sponsler. About this time Uncle Sam wrote a book on church history, which is still used as a guide in classes today.

After being at the school for some time, Uncle Sam felt he had one more missionary journey to make while he was still able. This was one journey I got to make with them. With the fire of an evangelist still burning in his soul, we started out. Our goal was to visit every relative of Uncle Sam's who was not in the church. We covered several states and many miles. We stopped at small cottages and large, palatial Southern homes. But in all of them the message was the same. Uncle Sam had come to tell them that the Lord was coming and they had better get their house in order before it was too late.

With this work done, Uncle Sam and Aunt Bessie returned to one of their early churches. The saints had wanted them to come back home. It wasn't long before Aunt Bessie went home to be with the Lord. A few more years and Uncle Sam went to join her.

To trace his life is to trace the history of our Pentecostal movement. Without men like Sam McClain, who had the faith and courage to pioneer, we would not be as far along our journey as we are today. His crown in glory will shine like the sun, because there will be a jewel in it for every church he had a part in helping.

Editor's note: According to S. C. McClain's obituary, he established over twenty Pentecostal churches in Arkansas, New Mexico, and Texas. The entire fellowship of the United Pentecostal Church is indebted to the fifty-seven years of fruitful ministry of this godly man. Hundreds of younger ministers have come under the influence of what he taught and the books he wrote.

Rev. and Mrs. S. C. McClain.

Bro. McClain built this church at 415 W. Taft Ave., Albuquerque, New Mexico.

Bro. McClain built this church at Arkadelphia, Arkansas.

16

STANLEY WARNER MCCONAGHY

by Joyce MacBeth Morehouse

On May 20, 1894, Stanley Warner, the eighth of nine children (five boys and four girls), was born to Andrew and Jane McConaghy. The McConaghys were Anglican but did not attend church regularly. Jane, an honest and upright lady, greatly influenced Stanley's later years.

Stanley disliked school and failed to get the type of education he needed. In his early twenties he got a job working in the coal mines of Minto, New Brunswick, Canada, living nearby at Rothwell. He got involved with drinking and other worldly activities, singing and playing the violin, and entertaining at dances.

Miss Murphy, a missions worker, visited the community to organize a Sunday school. Needing teachers, she asked Stanley if he would take a class. Never having been involved with a church, he refused at first, but later answered, "Well, if you can get my friend Henry Brown to help me, then I'll give it a try." Henry consented and for a while, with the assistance of the quarterly, they managed to get by. Before long, however, they ran into problems. "One Sunday our lesson was about Paul sitting at the feet of Gamaliel. I didn't know just what that was so I turned to my helper and said, 'Henry, what does Gamaliel mean? Is that a mountain?' Henry agreed that it must be."

Stanley played for the dances all week, then after teaching Sunday school in the morning, he played poker all afternoon. But he began to get concerned about his friends, and when he asked one young man, Mel Parker, to go to church with him the man called him a hypocrite. Not fully comprehending the word *hypocrite*, Stanley decided that Mel had "simply crossed the deadline and was beyond hope." Regardless of how drunk he was or what hour he came from the dance, however, Stanley knelt and said the Lord's Prayer.

When work at the mines slowed down, Stanley returned to Fredericton. Meantime, his father died, and before Christmas Stanley took typhoid fever. For three months he hovered between life and death in the hospital. His roommate, another young man with typhoid, died, as did also a nurse who had cared for them. As he confronted eternity, darkness and fear gripped his soul. A visiting minister asked, "How is it with your soul? Young man, you need to know!" But he failed to tell him what to do.

Faced with possible death, Stanley thought of the times he and a friend had made fun of Salvation Army street meetings. He had gotten a washtub, turned it upside down, beat on it, and then call his godless friends to testify. He had laughed and poked fun at the people's testimonies. As he recalled this, he prayed desperately, "Lord, if you'll forgive me and heal me, I'll serve You, but if You do not, I'll die trusting in Your mercy." He knew by the peace he felt that God had heard his cry. From that time he began to recover.

A few months later, Stanley married a lovely Minto girl, Lula Woods, but he forgot his promise to God and returned to his old lifestyle. The McConaghys had two sons, Tom and John, and a daughter, Muriel.

While Stanley worked as a shoe cutter at the Palmer shoe factory in Fredericton, the Reformed Baptist Church on King Street had special services with Lee Good from Maine. Lula went to the altar. One night Stanley decided to go along, and convicted of his ways, he remembered his promise to God. He could not sleep that night, so he knelt beside his bed, praying, "Lord, let me get to that altar tomorrow night and I'll serve You."

The next night he sat with Mel Parker. When the altar call was given, he rose with great difficulty and went forward. Beside him knelt a fifteen-year-old boy who was also to become a great pioneer of those early days—Clement Hyde. Stanley repented that night in 1924 and went home happy. He and Mel Parker poured forty bottles of home-brew down the sink. "Mind you, two old rum soaks with forty bottles of brew and throwing it all out," he recalled.

After throwing out his brew, he went to Uncle Sam's Secondhand Store and bought a Bible for a dollar so he could set up family altar. Together with other young converts-—George Delong, Clem Hyde, and Thomas Hoff— he began to seek the Holy Ghost, which had not yet been poured out in Fredericton. They witnessed in churches in Ripples, Hardwood Ridge, Minto, Midlands, and Fredericton, New Brunswick, as well as the state of Maine. Albert Thompson furnished a Model T Ford for their travels.

During the Depression years they hadn't much to travel on but prayer. Brother McConaghy recalled, "You'd think it was Pentecost! We had a hard time convincing people we were not 'Holy Rollers' but Reformed Baptists."

One Sunday, Charlie McQuarrie (Bliss McQuarrie's brother) said, "Stanley, there are some Pentecostal people having services in a tent on Woodstock Road."

"What do you mean by Pentecost?"

"Well, they believe in speaking in tongues."

"Speaking in tongues? Where do you get that?"

"It's in the Bible. Come on up and hear them."

Brothers Harvey, Charlie Flewelling, Earl Jacques, Wynn Stairs, and Clifford Crabtree, and the Davis Sisters, Susie and Caro, all sat on the platform. Stanley watched in amazement as Susie Davis shook under the power of God. They are certainly peculiar, he thought, but he was hungry for that power.

He and his friends sought it in the Reformed Baptist church. The zealous Reformed Baptists held services on Sundays. After McConaghy had preached one Sunday night, he spoke to a young man about coming to the altar. The young man just groaned. Not knowing too much about Holy Ghost conviction, Stanley left the young man groaning more than ever. A few years later, he met the man, Ellery Cady, again but this time he was baptized in Jesus' name, filled with the Holy Ghost, and preaching the gospel.

On another occasion Stanley McConaghy and his friends gathered in a pasture at Hardwood Ridge to pray for their night service when another young man, Bill Drost, happened by. He stopped, listened to their prayers, and was hounded by them until he later gave his heart to God.

Tribulation did not pass Stanley by. He continued to hunger for Holy Ghost, but Satan never gave up. First their eighteen-month-old baby, Douglas, took spinal meningitis and died within a few days. A little later Lula became ill with a lump on her neck, was told she had tuberculosis and spent over a year in the sanitorium at Riverglade.

Stanley still traveled around for meetings, even attending some Pentecostal services. One night in the service at Neil's Lane in Fredericton, he was asked to lead song service, and the blessing of the Lord came down. The saints danced, talked in tongues and praised the Lord. Later Stanley commented to Abby Staples (Verner Larsen's first wife), "It was like being in a beehive."

"Why didn't you raise your hands and praise God too?" she responded.

Stanley's wife came home from the hospital the next spring much improved. The lump in her neck left and she had gained weight. One evening she watched as Stanley prepared to go out, then asked, "Where are you going?"

"Over the river to be baptized in Jesus' name," he replied.

As he searched the Scriptures, the Lord dealt with him and convinced him of the truth of Jesus Name baptism. On the way, he met his Reformed Baptist friends, who asked, "Where are you headed?" They failed to understand his reasoning. "I thought you were already baptized," they argued, but he went on to Brother Jacques's house, where Brother Moody Wright was filling in for Brother Jacques, who was away for the summer. Brother

Wright gladly buried him in Jesus' name, and Stanley commented, "I went on my way rejoicing."

The Lord dealt with Stanley about preaching Jesus Name baptism at the Reformed Baptist services in Hardwood Ridge. First he resisted, thinking his friends would reject him, but then he stopped struggling and preached the message. "What a great message!" his friends said.

During this time, the McConaghys had a baby girl, Muriel. One morning when Stanley was preparing for work, he heard Lula call, "Stanley, you'd better not go to work today."

"Are you not feeling well, Lula?" he asked.

"No. Jesus is coming to take me away."

"Lula, don't you want to live?"

"Goodbye, Stanley. I'll meet you in heaven. Be good to the children. Jesus has come for me." Without a struggle Lula closed her eyes and was gone.

In his sorrow, Stanley's hunger for God intensified. He still went to the Baptist church, then one day God spoke to him. "If you want the Holy Ghost, you'll have to go where they believe it."

This was difficult for him to do, but several of his friends had already gone that way. Clem Hyde was seeking the Holy Ghost, and Stanley's alcoholic brother had been filled with the Spirit, so in 1928 he decided to make the Pentecostal church in Devon (Fredericton) his home church.

He went to a prayer meeting to seek the Holy Ghost. As he prayed, several prayed with him: Brother and Sister Biles, Sister Draper, and Brother Albert Stickles. Brother Stickles, who had just received the Holy Ghost, said, "Let the Lord have your tongue, brother." After he said this several times, Brother McConghy related, "I got very annoyed and went over by the organ to pray, but the Spirit had left me. As I tried to pray, the Lord spoke, 'Go over and put your arm around that brother and tell him you are sorry for what you said.'" Although it was hard, he walked over to Brother Stickles, and the minute he said it, the Holy Ghost hit him like a bolt of lightning. Later he joked, "No one had to say, 'Brother, let the Lord have your tongue.' What a time I had!"

Brother McConaghy's mother was too old to care for his children so he boarded them in Saint John. Almost overcome by loneliness, he found comfort in the Holy Ghost.

One day Clem Hyde approached him saying, "Let's go down and hold some services in Geary." "All right, Clem," Stanley agreed, then bought new shoes. He later told about the eventful trip down the river. "We went on the train to the road to Geary. Rain poured down on the open ferry, soaking us. The water ran down my clothes into my new shoes and we had to walk seven miles to the services. I sure had sore feet!"

About this time, they decided to have a convention at Fredericton, so they went to Saint John, bought some old sails, and had the ladies to make a tent. They pitched the tent on the other side of the river, and the Howard A. Gosses came for special services. He taught and she preached.

The Lord reminded Brother McConaghy about the miners he had worked with in the Minto area. "They need to be reached." He rented a hall at Newcastle Creek, but the women in the area protested. "We don't want this crazy miner talking to our men." Finally they forced him out of the hall. Meanwhile Clem Hyde joined him saying, "Let's rent a hall in Minto." Although they met opposition, they finally secured the community hall, but the night before services started, someone burned the hall. They went across town to Newcastle Bridge and met a disgruntled Baptist, Dan Langin, who no longer went anywhere. He let them have his store, despite his wife's objections. They remodeled it and started services. The miners came and revival broke out.

Brother McConaghy returned to Fredericton, but Brother Hyde stayed on as pastor. Later he turned the work over to Brother Samuel Steeves, who founded a Bible school and prepared many preachers for gospel work. Brother McConaghy continued to travel, going from Sussex, where he worked with Brother Hatt, to Tracy with Brother Jacques.

While he pastored in Geary in 1932 he decided to remarry. He had known Marie Betts, a fine Christian girl, for a number of years. Later he related the story. "One day in Fredericton I asked her if she would marry me and look after my children. I did not paint a very rosy picture of the future to her. I told her plainly what to expect. I was a poor Pentecostal preacher without a home, no furnishings, and no car to drive, but I would try to care for her and together we would trust the Lord to care for us. Well, she consented and I said, 'I'll be up to Fredericton on March 9 (Thursday), and we'll get Brother Jacques to marry us. It would be a quiet wedding. Say nothing to anyone and you can come back to Geary with me on Friday.'

"Well, the day in March rolled around. It rained, snowed, and blew. I thought, Only Marie knows, so maybe we can just put it off awhile, but I started to walk the seven miles through rain and sleet. I caught the train and landed at Fredericton, and what do you suppose? Marie had told a lot of folks, and they were waiting to have a church wedding for us."

Stanley spent the remainder of 1933 in Geary and then moved to a place called Jerusalem, where he pitched a tent. He spent the winter and started to build a tabernacle, but his plans fell through. In 1935 he moved to New Horton where several received the Holy Ghost. This began the work in Albert County.

The biggest event of the year for old-time preachers was the Newcastle Bridge convention. Everyone tried to be there for fellowship. Brother McConaghy wanted to go but had no car. On one of Brother Hyde's visits he wrote a letter to the Davis sisters in Saint John, asking for money for a car for Brother McConaghy. They sent forty dollars, and with another forty, which young John earned cutting pulp, they bought a used car.

Gas was the next problem. The gas gauge wasn't working, so using a stick to measure, they headed for Sussex. "If I can get to Sussex, Brother Burns will have me preach and give me a dollar or so." Although Brother Burns already had a speaker, he did give Brother McConaghy fifty cents. Rolly Thorne's dad invited them to dinner and gave them fifty cents, so they went on, stopping in Chipman for the night with Abby and Verner Larsen, who pastored there.

At the convention, John Tranquilla told Stanley that God had shown him that Stanley would be the next pastor at Millville. "But, brother, God hasn't spoken to me, so I'll have to pray about it," he replied. In spite of this response, Brother McConaghy went to Millville in 1935, and a breach was healed as the people drew together in unity.

In September of 1936, Pa and Ma Sweeny came to Millville for revival. Although they were trinitarians, while they were there, they saw the light on Jesus Name baptism and a great revival swept the area.

In spite of the great revival, the McConaghys' stay was not all sunshine. They rented Milford Stairs's home and were using a stove they had borrowed from him. One day he came by and said, "I'm going to Jim Hall's for dinner. When I return, have the stove ready to go." "But, Brother, we can't do that! We're already cooking dinner. The stove will never be cool in time to move it." In spite of this and Sister McConaghy's tears, they had the stove ready when Milford returned. They had even more difficulty replacing it. Before they found one that would work, they tried a total of nine stoves!

At Millville they had a great revival with Sister Jackson, who had worked with Brother Dearing in Bangor. Later she was the camp speaker at the Newcastle Bridge convention.

Then Wynn Stairs asked Stanley to go with him to Prince Edward Island. As they started home Brother Stairs said, "I hear Clem Hyde is having meetings in a church at Grey Rapids. Let's go the back way and come out at the church." When they arrived Brother Hyde spotted them and invited Brother Stairs to preach and Stanley to give an altar call, with the admonition, "Don't put too much pressure on." "When I took over I had one thought in mind—to get people to the Lord. I sang and told some of my stories and soon we had the whole congregation at

172

the altar, except two ladies."

While at Millville Brother McConaghy also held services at Waterville. When he returned from Prince Edward Island, he resigned his eight-year pastorate at Millville. Because he had eye trouble and had lost his sight in one eye, his family doctor, Dr. Jewett, advised him, "Go to the specialist in Fredericton." Dr. Ross Wright advised surgery but Dr. Jewett said, "Go to Montreal for a second opinion." They decided to operate. Dr. Jewett told the surgeon, Dr. Took, about Brother McConaghy's circumstances and the surgeon did not bill him.

Although Brother McConaghy still lived in Millville, he now pastored in Waterville. The owner of his house wrote that on a particular day he wanted him out of the house. During this wartime, houses were hard to rent. When Brother McConaghy mentioned that he needed a house, someone spoke up, "I know where you can get a house cheap." It turned out that two houses were built back to back. The owner had sold one but the other had to be moved, so Brother McConaghy bought it and also some land. He put a cement basement under it and finally got moved in before winter.

While pastoring here, he held meetings for Brother Stanley in Bristol, Connecticut, and visited Andrew Urshan's church in New York. New York delighted him. "I was like Alice in Wonderland after coming out of the woods of New Brunswick to this city of lights, tall buildings, and underground streets."

When he returned home, he went to help Brother Jacques on King Street in Fredericton. While there, he got word that his wife had received a call from Leonard Parent in Michigan inviting him there. So he went for twenty-nine days (the maximum for a Canadian visitor at that time). A great revival broke out. When he got home he received a call from George Cook of Foxboro, Massachusetts, wanting him to come there. He went, with similar results, but before he got home, his brother Douglas had died in Fredericton.

In 1945 he became pastor in Woodstock, then in 1961 he moved to Doaktown to pastor. He retired in 1966 but continued to work on the district paper, *The Family Circle*, which he had started in 1957. He had his own column, "Down Memory Lane," from which many of these excerpts are taken.

On August 15, 1971, while his wife Marie held his hand, Brother McConaghy slipped peacefully away. Marie was at his side through most of his illness from the fall of 1970. In like manner she had stood by him through many hardships and trials in those early days of Pentecost. In addition to the two sons and one daughter of his first marriage, she had borne him three sons, Donald, Gerald, and Stanley, and two daughters, Shirley and Ruth.

Wynn Stairs preached Stanley McConaghy's funeral on August 18 at the Pentecostal church in Fredericton, a fitting location, for he had first repented in the Baptist church in this area and spent most of his time winning friends and ministering here.

Stanley and Marie McConaghy, 1934.

Stanley W. McConaghy

Rev. and Mrs. L. H. Michael

17

LEONARD H. MICHAEL

by Maureen Michael

The old barn with its debris of leftover corn and oats bore no resemblance to a stained-glass sanctuary where one might expect to meet Jesus Christ. But this was no ordinary experience that happened to thirty-nine-year-old L. H. Michael, who had been reared by a mother who believed miracles no longer occur. On July 31, 1930, the Holy Ghost was poured out on Brother Michael as he prayed in his barn. God seemed to demonstrate His power in a special way, for as Brother Michael began to speak in a heavenly language, God miraculously raised him bodily three times with only his heels touching the floor and then each time returned him gently to the floor. Never again did Brother Michael doubt the miraculous power of God.

It all began a year earlier in July 1929, when C. E. Carter came to the small town of Randolph, west of Paoli, Oklahoma. He built a brush arbor and preached for three weeks. L. H. Michael was the only convert in this meeting. Later he was baptized in water in the name of Jesus, a form of baptism unheard of in the local churches. In July a year later C. P. Kilgore came to Paoli and preached, proclaiming the same truth as preached earlier by Brother Carter. At this time Brother Michael received the fullness of the message as he prayed in his barn.

An elderly prayer warrior, Sister Combs, influenced Brother Michael also. He listened many times as she prayed hour after hour while he plowed in his fields nearby. He was a man whose pipe was his god. One of the grocers related that Prince Albert tobacco topped his grocery list. Although small, he got so angry once that he felled a mule with a single blow of his right fist. He was full of courage. His son describes him as "mean enough to fight for his rights yet compassionate enough not to prosecute the youths who stole his Rhode Island red chickens; obstinate enough to not back off an inch from anyone or anything; considerate enough to be afraid of offending others."

Shortly after he received the Holy Ghost, his new experience received a severe test when one of his sons failed to return home on schedule. Driving a Model T Ford, Brother Michael started searching for the youngster. A few miles from home, he had a flat tire. He had no spare. The "old man" would have spent time cursing fate, but now he merely removed the tire, threw it in the car, and resumed his journey. A few more miles produced a second flat and then a third. He returned home on three rims and one tire, with the lost child!

In March 1930 God called Brother Michael into the ministry. Although not an audible voice, his call was direct and forcible when God asked him as He had Peter, "Do you love Me?" For over forty-one years thereafter, he proved that, yes, he loved the Lord. His wife, Roxie Bell Craddock Michael, received the Holy Ghost in 1931 and worked faithfully with him. Seven children were born to this couple: Levoy, Ernest, Herbert, Wanda, June, Elden, and Ronald.

They learned early to sacrifice. When Brother Michael sent his two youngest sons to gather fruit or vegetables to take to their pastor, he said, "Boys, gather the largest you can find. We'll use the small ones." Brother Carter responded, "God bless the little ravens." As was common in the early thirties, funds were low. Evangelists received little or no compensation. In one such revival at a home missions work the total offering was eleven cents.

Although he was an evangelist, Brother Michael pastored several years. Elmore City, Oklahoma, was an early pastorate. A seven-week revival here reaped forty-six who were baptized in Jesus' name and twenty-six who received the Holy Ghost. The family lived in the church while holding services under a combination brush arbor and tent. A son remembers what a treat it was to drink Kool Aid three times a day. He also remembers picking cherries to be sold in order to buy gas for their 1931 Buick.

Brother Michael also pastored in Paoli, Pauls Valley, and Allen, Oklahoma. He evangelized in Oklahoma, Arkansas, Mississippi, and Texas.

The spirit of sacrifice never left Brother Michael, even when he was hospitalized. During this time he gave a sacrificial offering to help build a home missions church. He also became distraught that he was no longer able to go to the church at six o'clock each morning to pray as had been his custom for many years. But during this time, God gave him a reassuring vision.

Brother Michael felt that some of his efforts were successful and others seemingly a failure, but he always trusted that in the final reckoning perhaps more good would be revealed. At his death, six ministers who came to the Lord under his ministry were his pallbearers. The presiding minister was also his convert.

The Michaels died within two weeks of each other. Brother Michael's homecoming was September 21, 1972, and two weeks later, on October 4, Sister Michael joined him. Their son Eldon remarked, "I wonder if Papa met her at the gate." The inscription on their tombstone, designed by their children, sums up the devotion of this couple: "Devoted in life, together through the ages."

18

BENJAMIN HARRISON PEMBERTON

by Roger Bailey

On March 24, 1891, Kelles Jasper and Julia Ann Pemberton were at their home in Edgewood, Illinois, awaiting the family doctor. Just a quarter of a mile away, the old country doctor was driving his horse and buggy up the small dirt road. "Get along now, Dolly, we must hurry a bit. Things like this can't wait on time or tide. Reckon this is about the sixth time I have visited the K. J. Pembertons with a youngster. Must be getting pretty crowded up there in that little house by now."

When he reached the tiny log cabin, K. J. was waiting outside. "Go on in, Doc. I'll take care of your horse," said K. J.

Wasting no time, the doctor rushed into the room where Mrs. Pemberton was and delivered the smallest "squirming bit of humanity" he had ever seen, a boy weighing just two and a half pounds. Kelles Jasper and Julia Ann, both Republicans and politically minded, named the newborn after the president, Benjamin Harrison.

Six years later, three more children had been added to the family. Benjamin, like most children, was energetic and could often be found playing or wrestling with his siblings and friends.

Although his family lived in Edgewood, they socialized and shopped in the town of Iola. It was located up the road and was central to most of the surrounding area.

At the age of seven, while Benjamin was walking in the woods, the Lord spoke to him with words of promise. He told Benjamin that he would reach many people with the gospel, and this thrilled Benjamin's soul for a long period of time. However, several events eventually caused Benjamin to forget the promise he had received.

When Benjamin was in the fifth grade, one of his brothers died, and his father became ill. Benjamin quit school and helped the family with farming. This transition in life caused Benjamin to seek manhood and forget about his childhood play. He started hanging around rough kids and drinking almost every night. Things continued this way until Benjamin's brother Granvil gave news of work in Arkansas. They both spent a couple of years working there until Benjamin felt the need to return home.

Benjamin's family had attended a trinitarian Pentecostal church since his youth. It was located in Byers' Grove and was the first church established there by the Byers family. After Benjamin's return, however, he continued drinking and carousing as he had before.

In 1909, evangelists Fred and Harry Blunt came to Iola from Arkansas. Benjamin was impressed with the large crowds that gathered to hear these brothers and decided to go find out what was so interesting about them. He was later baptized, along with several of his family members, by Harry Blunt, and he received the Holy Ghost. By 1913, Benjamin had regained his childhood desire to reach souls with the gospel of Christ and preached his first sermon at the church in Byers' Grove. During his message, the Lord told Benjamin to go to St. Louis, where he would find guidance in yielding to Him.

Kelles Jasper was upset with his son's decision because he felt there were enough "jack-legged" preachers going around. This was the common term used for insincere men who tried to claim the call of God to preach.

Without his father's blessing, Benjamin left for St. Louis with his Gospel of St. John in hand. Before he left town, however, a neighbor lady approached him and told of how the Lord instructed her to give him the address of one of her friends, Mother Moise.

Maria Christina Gill Moise conducted a training home for Christian workers during the last twenty years of her life. Prior to this, she ran a rescue home for wayward girls on North Eleventh Street. The St. Louis Police Department held high regard for Mother Moise and often sent runaways to her. In fact, she was given first prize at the 1904 World's Fair for her devoted help in the community.

However, in 1913, Mother Moise became ill and sought the Lord for someone to take over her responsibilities. She expected someone with wealth and culture, as she had been, to be converted and sent. But God's ways are not our ways and Mother Moise was soon to find this out.

Upon his arrival at St. Louis, Benjamin went to 2829 Washington Avenue. Mrs. Hunger, the housekeeper, answered the door. "Is this Mother Moise's home?" asked Benjamin. "I was sent here by Mrs. Woolridge." Mrs. Hunger stated that Mother was ill but invited Benjamin to stay for lunch.

After Benjamin prayed over the meal, the Spirit fell on everyone at the table. Mother Moise could hear the commotion from her upstairs room and inquired who in the world was making so much noise.

The workers took Benjamin to Mother's room, where he prayed for her. She was healed instantly. The Lord spoke to Mother Moise, "This boy is another David. He needs much training, but I will tear down everything in him." Mother's prayer was finally answered.

Mother's curriculum for Benjamin was washing, ironing, scrubbing, helping with general repairs, and of course, studying the Bible and praying. The menial tasks were not what Benjamin thought acceptable for an ambitious young minister who was called of God, but he swallowed his pride and agreed to cooperate.

Mother, Benjamin, and about six others met every night at the mission halls for services. Their offerings seldom accumulated over fifteen cents. Benjamin brought a new experience to Pentecost that Mother was not accustomed to, though, for he kept order within the services by throwing out anyone who disturbed them. His preaching was also impressive for such a young person, and sinners were coming from all over to hear this anointed man.

The *St. Louis Post Dispatch* did a big write-up and nicknamed Benjamin "Brother Ben." Of course, this term was intended sarcastically, but it furnished Benjamin with an easy way for all members and newcomers to remember him by.

As a young man at the home, Brother Ben conducted many evangelistic meetings with large crowds and had great success in getting people to turn to God. After some time, he gained confidence in his own ability and even thought about leaving the home. While preaching at an Illinois meeting, the Lord asked him if he desired to be an Esau with a worldly and prosperous following, or did he prefer to be a Jacob who had the spiritual birthright and was blessed in the Spirit. Brother Ben decided to choose the way of Jacob, and that meant returning to Mother Moise in St. Louis and being instructed in the way of the Spirit.

This particular Illinois meeting was in a new field for the Pentecostal message. Local hoodlums would throw stones during the services, and Satan tried to prevent any success on the last night of this meeting. However, victory came when twenty people were gloriously filled with the Holy Ghost.

In 1914, the doctrine of Oneness and Jesus Name baptism began to grow rapidly on the West Coast. Mother Moise and Brother Ben, being trinitarians, prayed that it would not spread to the Midwest. At this time, the Assemblies of God had their headquarters in St. Louis on 2800 Easton Avenue, and some of the officials from this organization were living in Mother Moise's home. Also during this time, Mother Moise, Brother Ben, and others held services at a hall on 3032 Olive Street.

Mother Moise began receiving tracts on Jesus Name baptism and the Godhead as well as a religious magazine published by Elder Frank J. Ewart of Los Angeles. Brother Ewart and Glenn Cook were among the first to be baptized in the name of Jesus and to acknowledge Jesus Christ as the one God in the flesh.

Midwestern trinitarians became even more discouraged, so they prayed fervently against the successful move of the Oneness message. There were even times when Mother Moise, Dr. E. N. Bell (chairman of the Assemblies of God), and Brother Ben would devise a plan of attack against the "Jesus Only" crusaders.

A few weeks later, Glenn Cook visited Mother Moise's home on a Friday evening. He was on his way to Indiana, but he stopped in St. Louis, for he knew Brother Ben. A young girl answered the door, and when she heard him say, "I am Glenn Cook of Los Angeles, from Elder Frank J. Ewart's church," she ran upstairs to Mother Moise's room and broke the news to her. That day, Mother Moise and Brother Ben spoke with Brother Cook concerning the Oneness doctrine. Brother Cook stayed at the home until Sunday afternoon, because Mother Moise had asked him to preach for their Sunday morning service.

Sunday services were always held at the home, starting at 10:30 A.M., and at this particular service were E. N. Bell and Roswell Flower, secretary of the Assemblies of God. Brother Cook chose Acts 2:38 as his text and preached water baptism in Jesus' name, using other verses of Scriptures as well. Brother Ben watched Brother Bell and noticed the upset look on his face and how he squirmed uncomfortably in his chair.

Eventually, right in the midst of Brother Cook's sermon, Brother Bell stood up and shouted, "Brother, you are in error! Read Matthew 28:19 where it says, 'Go ye into all the world, baptizing them in the name of the Father, and of the Son, and of the Holy Ghost.'"

Following his outburst, a debate broke out that lasted for three hours. Brother Bell was much disturbed afterwards and immediately left for Tennessee. Brother Ben, being convinced of the sermon, asked Brother Cook to

186

baptize him. So they went to the Mississippi River, where Brother Ben became the first to be baptized in Jesus' name in the Midwest. Mother Moise and others were not rebaptized until later, when evangelist L. C. Hall of Zion City came.

After his victory in St. Louis, Brother Cook traveled to Indianapolis, Indiana, where he baptized Elder G. T. Haywood and Elder L. V. Roberts. E. N. Bell later saw the light and asked L. V. Roberts to come to Tennessee to baptize him, but he did not stay with this message.

Mother Moise and Brother Ben remained forever grateful to Brother Cook. Brother Ben experienced his personal revelation of Jesus Christ as the mighty God through reading about the Israelites in I Corinthians 10:4: "For they drank of that spiritual Rock that followed them: and that Rock was Christ."

After the summer months, Brother Ben returned to the mission halls and storefronts. Continually moving the chairs, benches, and instruments was a tiresome task, but Brother Ben was willing to do anything for the cause of Christ.

Several of Brother Ben's mission halls were in buildings where lodge gatherings occurred, such as the Old Moose Hall on Grand and West Pine. This particular hall was rented out to the Ku Klux Klan at the same time Brother Ben was there. Brother, Ben never dealt with such private organizations, but when his services began, the other accompanying lodge halls would be emptied, and the people would all go hear the fiery young preacher. A doctor whose office was behind Brother Ben's hall never actually attended the meetings, but he made a hole in the wall and sat with his ear next to it. He was later converted to the cause of Christ.

During a tent meeting in 1922, the St. Louis police had to come out and direct traffic. This big tent was located on Vandeventer and Evans Avenue, and a thousand people showed up one night. At one service, Brother Ben aroused much excitement and fear in everyone present. He reached such a state of exaltation that he climbed the center tent pole, and while hanging upside down on the crossbar, he shouted "Glory, Glory!" He also performed another common stunt by jumping over the pulpit rail, dashing down the middle aisle to the street, doing a couple of handsprings, and jumping right back in the pulpit. He also raised four hundred dollars that night for his church building fund.

However, Brother Ben lost part of his congregation that year to someone who came through and preached that believers could avoid death and have eternal life on earth. Unfortunately, Mother Moise accepted this doctrine, and at this time, Brother Ben felt the need to take his flock and go elsewhere.

Brother Ben had given his all to Mother Moise's school and left with only a dime in his pocket. However, by the end of 1922, the Lord had blessed him with two hundred followers and a desire to start his own church. From Mother's home, Brother Ben moved into the Sir Walter Raleigh Apartments on Washington Avenue, where he remained for many years.

The last mission hall that Brother Ben and his congregation occupied before going into their first church was at 1414 North Grand. Brother Ben was a great businessman and saved almost every penny for God's work. He wore cheap clothing and sacrificed the mere comforts of life. He remained close friends with Mother Moise and even considered his own ministry as a continuation of hers. Truly, the years spent with her were not in vain, for now he knew how to seek God and trust in Him.

In 1924, Brother Ben purchased a lot at 4017 Easton Avenue. A large brick building was immediately constructed that seated eight hundred people. Once again, stories and pictures were printed by the *Old Times* and *St. Louis Post Dispatch* about Brother Ben's new home.

Services were held every night with standing room only during the weekends. Not even the Depression seemed to weaken the church. In 1929, the church's bank closed, and only part of the church's money was refunded to Brother Ben, but a peculiar blessing occurred for his congregation. None of them lost their jobs or had to apply for relief. In fact, the church created a poor fund for those in need.

Once a family without food or money came to the church. Brother Ben immediately gave to them. He decided to visit the family later that day and arrived just as they sat down to supper. They had bought large steaks and fresh strawberries. From that time on, the church's policy changed: the church itself bought the food.

In 1917, Brother Ben became a member of the General Assembly of the Apostolic Assemblies, a Oneness ministerial organization that existed for only one year. By 1925, Brother Ben, along with W. H. Whittington, led a group of ministers in St. Louis under the title of Apostolic Churches of Jesus Christ. Two years later at a joint convention held in Guthrie, Oklahoma, the Apostolic Churches of Jesus Christ merged with Emmanuel's Church in Jesus Christ. The elected officials were Ben

Pemberton, chairman; W. H. Lyon, vice chairman; W. H. Whittington, secretary and foreign missions secretary; and J. O. White, treasurer. The following year, Oliver F. Fauss became chairman and Brother Ben was elected assistant chairman. The new organization was formed under the name Apostolic Church of Jesus Christ. Brother Ben later resigned from his office for reasons unknown.

On February 1, 1932, Brother Ben obtained credentials with the Pentecostal Assemblies of Jesus Christ, an organization formed by a merger between the Pentecostal Assemblies of the World and the Apostolic Church of Jesus Christ. Its first annual conference was held at Brother Ben's church on Easton Avenue from August 30 to September 4. Brother Ben remained with this organization until 1937, when he resigned, never to join a religious body again.

By 1940, the neighborhood around 4017 Easton Avenue had gotten too rough for Brother Ben's congregation, so they began seeking the Lord for a new location. During a Wednesday afternoon prayer meeting, the Lord told Brother Ben, "Get up, for you have your new place." He immediately announced the good news, and everyone stood to give God the glory. However, the Lord did not specify where this "new place" was.

Brother Ben set out to find his new church home and noticed the Fountain Park Christian Church for sale, but his attempt to buy it was unsuccessful. Waiting on the Lord's direction, Brother Ben and his congregation grew in their desire for a new location, until one morning the Lord told Brother Ben to offer fifteen thousand dollars cash for a place on Delmar Street. It had been a nightclub named the Capri Inn but was now a car garage and in bad condition. Brother Ben also knew that it had been taken over by the government and had a large loan on it. Unexpectedly, his small offer was accepted, even in the face of greater ones.

Much time was spent on rehabilitating the new church, especially on trying to get the grease spots off the concrete floors. An apartment was built and furnished for Brother Ben on the second floor. The church was considered a credit to the neighborhood, and all the area newspapers came out for a write-up. Dickson Terry, the *Post-Dispatch's* feature writer said, "Brother Ben's church looks like a modern painting in a cold water flat." The building seated 1,400 people. It had carpeted prayer rooms and a small auditorium for weeknight services.

After the move was completed, several members formed a committee to start a monthly publication. These papers usually included a sermon by Brother Ben, testimonials, a children's page, and general announcements.

On March 24, 1950, the church had a special service for Brother Ben's birthday and presented him with a check for a new car. Many of his friends from all over the country attended this event.

Shortly before May of 1951, Brother Ben started a radio ministry and preached each Sunday on WTMV. During that month, however, he was moved to a new station, KSTL, because of his good ratings. Many people found the Lord through Brother Ben's radio ministry. Brother Ben often prophesied on the radio, and the station owner consistently threatened that if any of the prophecies did not come to pass, then Brother Ben would be "out the door." Apparently, the owner did not realize that Brother Ben's prophecies were actually from God.

In 1953, Brother Ben felt the Lord's impression to move his congregation to a more central area of the city. He later bought an old Methodist church located at 3610 Grandel Square. The church family pitched in to clean, paint, and prepare the new building for Pentecostal worship.

The new church had three auditoriums: a large sanctuary with a balcony, a smaller one on the third floor, and the smallest auditorium just off the foyer. An addition was built, made with matching limestone, that served as Brother Ben's apartment. Janitorial and evangelist quarters were also furnished along with Sunday school rooms and a secretary's office located under the belfry.

Brother Ben's career as a minister was nothing less than successful. His congregation was composed of men, women, and children who all knew how to worship and pray to their God.

Services were still held every night except for Monday. Friday night was youth service with all the young people dancing and singing, and Brother Ben danced right along, beating his tambourine. Prayer service was held before each service, but the "cry rooms" were open at all times for anyone who needed them.

Lyman Price, a St. Louis police sergeant, was a true friend to his pastor. He comforted and nursed Brother Ben during his sicknesses.

Grace Mueller was Brother Ben's personal secretary for approximately twenty-five years. She and her family first encountered Brother Ben when she was nine years old and they attended his church on Easton Avenue. Sister Grace undertook many church responsibilities, such as taking charge of providing special meals for

Brother Ben during his last fifteen years of life. He had become a diabetic and refused to take any insulin, but he gave God and the women of his church the credit for keeping him alive.

Ethyl Dickey served as another right hand of Brother Ben's. She had overheard one of Brother Ben's tent meetings on Grand Avenue in 1921. Impressed with the lively and joyous music, she decided to attend and later became the church choir director, writer of the "Time Clock" in the church paper (concerning biblical prophecy), and director of the youth service.

Brother Ben never married. He related the story of the time he was praying at a church family's home while the children were playing and tripping over his legs. The Lord then said, "You cannot give your all to Me and have children too." So Brother Ben, like Paul, remained unmarried and faithful to the cause of Christ. He considered his church as his family and always spent special occasions with someone from his congregation.

A couple of the many great ministers who came out of Brother Ben's church were Walter S. Guinn and Benjamin H. Hite. These men adopted Brother Ben's burden for St. Louis and established their own works there.

In 1963, a large celebration was held in honor of Brother Ben's fiftieth year in the ministry. Judge Scott was the main speaker and highly acclaimed the man of God who obeyed the call to preach in St. Louis. It was a great experience for Brother Ben to see many of his lifelong friends and converts who had moved away.

That same year, however, Brother Ben's congregation became concerned by a frequent statement that Brother Ben made. He prophesied that blood would soon be on the street and that the nation would be in total anguish as a result. He also told several individuals that he too would be with his Maker before this tragedy would occur. His prophecy was fulfilled in the death of President John F. Kennedy on November 22.

Around 1,800 people attended Brother Ben's funeral. Much could be said about the wonderful things that his good friends and church family had to share, but an interesting story was related by Nathaniel Urshan, general superintendent of the United Pentecostal Church International and personal friend of Brother Ben's.

Brother Urshan had arrived at Union Station and was taking a cab to Brother Ben's church. When he told the cab driver the address, the driver said, "Oh, that's good old Brother Ben's church." He went on to tell of the time when he did not have a job and Brother Ben got him on with the cab company. Brother Ben hardly knew the man, but he sensed the feelings of despair and did all he could to help him.

"Are you visiting his church?" the cab driver asked Brother Urshan. "No, I'm preaching his funeral," stated Brother Urshan. "Do you think I could come to pay my respects also?" asked the driver. "Sure you can," said Brother Urshan. So he parked his cab and stayed for the service.

Benjamin Harrison Pemberton was an overcomer. He told many before his death that he had finally conquered his old flesh and was under total submission to his Savior. In fact, one of Brother Ben's common statements was, "Overcome everything that confronts you, whether it be large or small, for there is no promise in the Bible but to an overcomer."

194

Brother Ben's tabernacle in 1932.

Benjamin Harrison Pemberton

Brother Ben in his church.

19

T. RICHARD REED

by Vernita Craine Reed

"Oh, Lord, You know about Richard. He is at the age when he must make decisions for his future. Help him to surrender his life to you, Lord. Help him make the right decisions." Coming home from school one day, teen-aged Richard overheard his mother talking to Someone—visitors? Hesitating to listen, he realized his mother was talking to God about him. This prayer, no doubt, changed the course of his life.

On May 26, 1911, when redbud and dogwood trees bloomed, the cry of a newborn baby interrupted the medley of the birds' spring song on the Reed farm. A ten-year-old girl, Mabel, looked at the black bag the doctor carried, then at the new baby boy, and wondered, "Where did that baby come from?" Thomas Richard was the name chosen for the Reed's third son: Thomas came from his father's name and Richard was for the doctor. Mabel and his big brothers, Charles and Tim, admired the baby as did Mom and Dad, Beulah and Tom Reed.

The Reed family moved later to a cotton farm across the road from the railroad and one mile from Corning,

Arkansas. Here another baby son, Shanno, joined the family. C. P. Kilgore pastored the First Pentecostal Church of Corning, where Mother Reed attended. Brother Kilgore held an open-air meeting a few miles from Corning. T. Richard Reed, then fifteen years old, was the only one who prayed through in that meeting. The stars shone brighter over the cotton fields as he rode home.

In his last year of high school, his psychology teacher made a derogatory remark about the Pentecostal religion. After the session the entire class went to the teacher and demanded that he recant his statements about Pentecost or, "We'll not come back to your class. Our class president, Richard, is Pentecostal." The teacher apologized.

On April 2, 1927, sixteen-year-old Richard preached his first sermon, from I Timothy 4:12: "Let no man despise thy youth; but be thou an example of the believers, in word, in conversation, in charity, in spirit, in faith, in purity." He graduated with honors from Corning High School in 1929.

On August 4, 1929, the First Pentecostal Church of Corning elected T. Richard Reed as pastor. The Lord blessed his ministry, giving him favor in the community. Rowdy teens tested the young pastor when they tried to disrupt the services. Officers of the law arrested the youths for disturbing the peace.

While pastoring his first church, Brother Reed began his radio ministry. On July 7, 1934, he aired his first broadcast over KBTM, Paragould, Arkansas, called "Saturday Afternoon Devotional." The radio station soon moved to Jonesboro, which meant a 130-mile round trip on a gravel road.

In 1936-37 Brother Reed was elected national president of the Pentecostal Gleaners, the youth department of the Pentecostal Church, Incorporated. His busy pastoral schedule now included promotional travel to other states.

His eight years of pastoring in Corning included some unique experiences. L. H. Benson, superintendent of the Tennessee District, tells how Brother Reed carried him, a visiting young evangelist, on his shoulders across a creek.

The First Pentecostal Church of Trumann, Arkansas, called Brother Reed as pastor in 1937. Right away he had to preach a double funeral for a couple, a case of murder-suicide on the sidewalks of that rough, lumber mill town.

Following a baptismal service in a dredge ditch, a big burly fellow bragged that if Brother Reed baptized his wife, he would kill him, pulling a revolver out of his pocket to make his point. When the man saw his wife floating on the water (blessed and overcome by the Holy Spirit after her baptism), he was convinced that a "Higher Power" had control. "I'd better keep my hands off. My wife cannot swim or float. She's afraid of water." Brother Reed rejoiced to see the man in the altar that night weeping his way to repentance.

While in Trumann, God gave Brother Reed a burden for Jonesboro, where there was no Pentecostal church. In 1942 he opened the Bible Hour Tabernacle in Jonesboro. It became the center of his radio work, and the "Blessed Old Bible Hour" eventually aired over both KBTM and KLCN, reaching thirteen states.

An eligible bachelor, Brother Reed did not have a helpmate. This changed, however, when the Craine family moved to Jonesboro. Brother Clarence Craine responded to Brother Reed's request to come and help with his new venture of faith, not dreaming that one year and three months later he would consent to give him one of his daughters for a bride. On a hot summer day Pastor Reed first visited the Craine family. Vernita was ironing and had kicked off her shoes. When she saw the pastor walk upon the front porch, she blushed as she scrambled for her sandals.

On August 29, 1944, the barefoot girl of the Ozarks became her new pastor's bride. The newlyweds held their first revival a month later in Finley, Tennessee. A big tent behind the church was the setting for a three-week meeting. A couple of Sunday school rooms served as living quarters for the evangelists. Ninety-five people knelt in the sawdust and prayed through to the Holy Ghost.

In October 1944 the last conference of the Pentecostal Church, Incorporated (before the merger that formed the United Pentecostal Church) was held in Jonesboro at the Bible Hour Tabernacle with Brother Reed as host pastor. The Reeds' first child, a son, was born January 30, 1952. After waiting for almost eight years for this blessed event, Brother Reed announced the birth on his radio broadcast. Thomas Richard Reed was called Rickey.

That fall Brother Reed took his first trip to the Holy Land, a six-week seminar of the Winona Lake School of Theology, studying the Bible in the land of its origin. Afterwards he conducted twelve such tours, receiving one free trip along with other tour hosts from the Ministry of Tourism of Israel.

In the spring of 1953 the Arkansas District elected Brother Reed as district superintendent. He held that office for six years. During this time he engineered the relocation of the Arkansas District campground, moving it from Mt. Crest, a very difficult mountaintop location with no modern facilities, to Redfield. Many people wondered, however, if they would ever be able to get a "mountaintop" experience if they left the mountain!

The Reeds' second son, Robert Michael, arrived on November 4, 1953. Before he left for a Sunday school convention Brother Reed sent his wife one dozen roses; he returned just in time to check his wife and son out of the hospital. On January 13, 1956, Samuel Timothy Reed arrived.

With his growing family, Brother Reed realized that his duties as superintendent demanded his being away from home and church almost two-thirds of the time, so he resigned this position and his church and accepted a call to Laurel, Mississippi, to pastor the First Pentecostal Church. The Reeds remember their first spring in Laurel with azaleas as tall as the eaves of the house blooming profusely.

The daughter of their dreams arrived October 5, 1960. The nurses at the hospital reported that they had never seen such a happy father! First child? No, first daughter.

One day the telephone rang in the parsonage; the Tennessee District superintendent, W. M. Greer, was calling. He told Brother Reed of a church in Memphis in need of a pastor. "I'll pray about it," Brother Reed promised. During the Thanksgiving holidays in 1962 the Reeds moved to Memphis.

The First Pentecostal Church in Memphis was not in a nice brick building like the one in Laurel; the unfinished huge monstrosity of a building was dubbed the "bomb shelter." Kneeling in the altar one Sunday the pastor's wife was embarrassed upon arising—the hem of her crepe dress rose too. She had knelt in a puddle of water from the leaky roof!

Pastor Reed searched for a more desirable location for the church and found a building at 1915 Young Avenue in the heart of the city. "In the heart of Memphis with Memphis at heart" was the slogan chosen for the church news published by *Memphis Mirror* (All Church Press). The First United Pentecostal Church met to worship in their new church for the first time on July 7, 1963. It was organized with ninety charter members, and Superintendent Greer set the church in order. Purchased from Lamar Heights Presbyterian Church, the building had no baptistry, so Johnny Sparks and Dan Webb soon installed one. Among the first six baptized was the pastor's youngest son, Sammy, who had received the Holy Ghost just a few weeks earlier.

In March 1964 the Sunday school attendance increased seventy-five percent over the year before, winning the first place award in the state.

"Second Sunday Gospel Singing"—two hours of singing by quartets, duets, solos, ensembles, and choirs of local churches—was broadcast live from the church on the second Sunday afternoon every month for eight years. The "Blessed Old Bible Hour" was heard over KSUD every Sunday afternoon from 2:00 to 2:30. After many years the time was changed to Sunday morning from 8:00 to 8:30.

Brother Reed, a pioneer in radio gospel in his area, also served for ten years on the original radio committee of the United Pentecostal Church International that organized Harvestime, the international radio voice of the

U.P.C.I. Later he served as Harvestime representative for the Tennessee District.

The Tennessee District in April 1968 elected Brother Reed as presbyter for his home section. He served the Memphis area as presbyter for seventeen years, resigning in 1985, but then becoming an honorary member for life.

During fifty-six years of pastoring, Brother Reed has served as "father in the Lord" to many called to minister. They include Bruce Allen, Owatonna, Minnesota; Joy Cooley, wife of C. E. Cooley, Tioga, Louisiana; G. D. Craine, Ft. Smith, Arkansas; Beulah and James Davis, Ludington, Michigan; Steve Evans, Arkansas; Eunice Howerton, Colono, Illinois; E. E. Jolley, Bessemer, Alabama; Rick McCarver, Memphis, Tennessee; Ernestine Norman, Heber Springs, Arkansas; James Rider, California; Jeff Sanders, Philadelphia, Pennsylvania; Vondas Smith and wife, La Paz, Bolivia; Nancy Holloway, wife of Pastor Keith Holloway, Alamo, Tennessee; Patricia Sandy, wife of Pastor Eddie Sandy, Southaven, Mississippi; Neoma Thomas, Yellville, Arkansas; Donald Whitt, Hot Springs, Arkansas; Basil Williams, Florida; Ralph Ezell, Jonesboro, Arkansas; Don Williams and wife, Lexington, Tennessee; Wayne Gilliland, Memphis, Tennessee. Brother, Reed likes to visit these pastors and their churches and meet some of his "grandchildren."

First Church, Young at Barksdale, grew spiritually and numerically, flourishing under Brother Reed's capable leadership. But no pastor works alone. Dedicated and consecrated people helped carry the load. Space does not permit naming each helper, including helpers with the radio work and ladies auxiliary. Each time a job transfer came or some of the youth (including his own children) married and left, Brother Reed visualized laborers going into the harvest instead of lamenting his loss.

Then moving day came for the church—not the pastor. An eight-year-old church was offered to Brother Reed in East Memphis, Mallory at Watson, by J. H. Ford, the pastor. The church members voted to accept the offer, put the older church up for sale, and buy the newer church in August 1980.

Added to all his other titles, on Thanksgiving Day, 1973, Brother Reed became a grandfather when Christina Michelle was born to Vicki and Mike Reed. Nine other grandchildren and two step-grandsons were added to the family tree, keeping it in full bloom.

July 21, 1984, a golden jubilee celebration honored Brother Reed for fifty years of continuous broadcasting on radio. A film entitled "Pilgrim's Progress" portrayed Pastor Reed's life. This was followed by a reception. The next day First Pentecostal Church celebrated its twenty-first anniversary and the last anniversary for Pastor Reed.

Brother Reed submitted his resignation as pastor December 30, 1984. He had suffered two strokes in January and August and felt unable to do what needed to be done, but he did continue to serve until the church elected a new pastor in March 1985. Brother James Sharp of Columbus, Ohio, took the helm as captain of the ship with Wayne Gilliland as assistant.

For the first time in fifty-six years Brother Reed was free from the responsibility of pastoring. He prayed for open doors to minister, for the desire to preach still burned within. Invitations came. The first year he ministered in twenty-seven churches in Tennessee, Alabama, and Arkansas.

The Yellville United Pentecostal Church in the Ozarks of Arkansas had been praying for revival. Brother Reed was invited for a weekend in April 1986. The first night two people received the Holy Ghost. The weekend extended to a full week. Four received the baptism and another person was filled in the baptistry as Pastor Neoma Thomas baptized her in the name of Jesus. Later another interested person prayed through.

When people refer to Brother Reed as being retired, he strongly declares that instead of being retired he is being "refired" to preach as long as he lives! As his wife, mother of his children, nurse, chauffeur, and secretary from 1944 to the present, I conclude that all glory and honor and praise belong to our Lord and Savior and soon-coming King for any accomplishment during the sixty-five years of ministry, both in the pulpit and over the airwaves, of this pioneer of the gospel.

Tent revival in Walnut Ridge, Arkansas, in 1941.

The last Pentecostal Church Incorporated (P.C.I.) conference held at Jonesboro, Arkansas 1941, Pastor T. Richard Reed. Among the ministers on the platform: Bro. Reed, Howard A. Goss, A. D. Gurley, A. O. Moore, E. J. Douglas, and Missionary Alice Sheets.

Wedding photo of the Reeds sent to radio listeners in 1944.

The Reed family: Lower left clockwise, Mike, Ray, Morris, Sam, Cyndie, Vicki, and Bro. and Sis. Reed.

Rev. and Mrs. T. Richard Reed celebrate their forty-sixth anniversary.

Rev. and Mrs. J. Harper Rose celebrate their golden anniversary.

20

JOSEPH HARPER ROSE

by Treajetta Streley

Joseph Harper Rose was born April 12, 1892, in Wellsville, Ohio. His parents, William and Matilda Tarr Rose, had four other children: Mary, Ella, Cora, and Harry.

Young Harper learned meat cutting from his father, a butcher. Mr. Rose got sick in 1904, and at twelve Harper shouldered the burden of the Richmond, Ohio, butcher shop and slaughterhouse, and took over the cattle buying. He and his sister Mary ran the family peddle-wagon route as their father lay dangerously ill.

Being a violinist in a group of music makers earned Harper entry to dances, socials, and parties in several nearby towns. One of his acquaintances, Earl Van Allen, offered a bulldog for sale that Harper decided to see. From that first visit to the Van Allen home grew the romance of his life. Joseph Harper Rose met Lottie Louella Van Allen, and they attended the Lisbon fair on their first date in 1912. They married in Chester, West Virginia, December 23, 1914, then set up housekeeping on Walnut Street in Richmond. Harper returned to the family meat market.

In September 1915 the newlyweds moved to the family farm, and with a single cow and a few sheep, began farming. Butter sales became a mainstay of the family budget and remained so through the arrivals of Ella May, an anniversary gift on December 23, 1915; Edith Marie on November, 17, 1918; and Dorothy Jean on September 6, 1920.

Early in 1923 the Rose brothers, Harper and Harry, bought an established butcher shop in Jewett, Ohio. The farm equipment and stock were sold, and the growing family moved to the apartment above the meat market. On March 30, 1923, a fourth daughter, Martha Esther, was born.

A gentle, loving father, Harper Rose worked long, long hours and often saw his daughters only in their beds at evening. He spurned punishment in favor of discipline, seasoned well with prayer and guidance from the Word. Each child felt so special that each considered herself his favorite.

Harper didn't know how much he wanted a son until July 15, 1925, when Paul William arrived, welcomed by his four sisters. In 1927 the Rose family moved from above the business to a large house on Main Street in Jewett. The slaughterhouse, meat market, and peddle wagon still supported the family. The family enjoyed summertime when the children got to go on the route with their adored Daddy. One night, quite late, Harper Rose returned from his day's labors to a slumbering house. He and Lottie wakened the children so they could enjoy a special treat—chocolate ice cream and Daddy.

Harper Rose found a good helpmate in Lottie. She

supported his every enterprise and valued his walk with God, his power in prayer, and his profound knowledge of the Word. If ever she felt he was bordering on error, however, she said so!

In one instance Brother Rose had a tremendous "revelation" and enthusiastically expounded his new "truth." She listened, then looked up and asked, "Where in the Word did you find that?" Harper looked very peculiar for a moment, then said softly, "Thank you! Oh, thank you, thank you!" Occasionally she reminded him that the Bible says, "Preach the word." This helped Pastor J. Harper Rose to fulfill his ministry for forty faithful years.

The family altar was sacred. Harper Rose repeatedly told his children that he was leading them in all the light he had, and cautioned that if God ever shed more light on the Scripture, it must be accepted and obeyed. He rarely went anywhere without his Bible. Midday found him at lunch at the back of the butcher shop, seated on a high stool, his meal before him and the Word in his hand. He lived the Word. An acquaintance once asked what he searched for and Harper Rose answered, "I'm seeing if I still love the Lord." The man demanded a better answer and Harper Rose readily replied, "The Bible says, 'If you love me, keep my commandments,' and so I want to be sure I know them all."

Into this faithful dedication came the opportunity to serve in greater fullness and truth. While delivering meat to a restaurant in Georgetown in 1932, Harper Rose first heard the message of Jesus Name baptism and the indwelling Spirit of God. Sister Dollie White, visiting from Short Creek, West Virginia, shared the scriptural truth of the mighty God in Christ. Through that testimony has grown the tremendous work in Harrison County, Ohio, and the surrounding area. After carefully searching the Scriptures, Harper Rose accepted the message and was baptized in Jesus' name by Brother Albert Waite in Bridgeport, Ohio, in 1933. In 1941, Ella May, Martha, Sister Louie Rose, and Edith received the Holy Spirit. Brother Rose prayed through to the Holy Ghost under the ministry of Evangelist Willie Lane Johnson.

Brother Rose had been a faithful member of the Presbyterian church. After his acceptance of greater truth, he was astounded to find out that his Presbyterian family and friends were not delighted in his experience. A close relative came into the meat market, railing against Harper, declaring him a disgrace, accusing him of heresy, and attacking him physically. Yet Harper never wavered.

Although he had loved and served the Lord from childhood, Harper Rose had been a pouter. When displeased, he clamped his jaw shut and refused to reveal what troubled him. This technique gave his dear wife a sick headache. But one blessed day the Lord took the pout away and put the Spirit in its place!

An extra blessing arrived to the Roses on November 21, 1934, when Joseph Hugh Rose, the delight of his parents, four sisters and brother, joined the family.

Family worship brought spiritual refreshing. I Peter 1:18-21 was read, emphasizing the precious blood of Jesus. Brother Rose loved to sing songs that glorified the name, and psalms were sung from the Presbyterian Psalter. Among the family favorites were Psalms 23, 45, 87, and 128. Young Hughie knew that by requesting Psalm 128 he could see the retribution due all his naughty pranks washed away in Mother's tears. There he also learned that his sins could be washed away in his heavenly Father's waters of baptism.

The first meeting of the Jesus Name Church of Jewett, Ohio, was held in a renovated barber shop and pool hall on November 4, 1945, under Pastor Rose with eight people attending. About that time D. J. White of Akron, Ohio, preached a tent revival in town. Mexican railroad laborers worked nearby, and during a service, a message in tongues was brought forth in Spanish. Railroad employees listening outside overheard and interpreted the message.

Brother Rose held meetings in a tent in Cherry Valley and at Leesville, and in a school building in Rumley, Ohio. Betty Yeager discovered through these meetings that there were other Jesus Name believers in Harrison County and became a part of the congregation of believers in Jewett. She and many members of her family are still a part of the church today.

God has blessed this congregation with growth since its beginning. Occasionally, however, no one but family sat before Pastor Rose as he preached. On one occasion as he preached to an empty church, a small girl asked, "Were you practicing, Mr. Rose?" But the original sanctuary soon overflowed, and they needed Sunday school space. The Jesus Name Church of Jewett was renamed the Apostles' Doctrine Church and affiliated with the United Pentecostal Church.

Brother Rose instituted an annual celebration of the Feast of Pentecost in 1953, a time of warm fellowship and food. He was a man of prayer, and the altar at church was his workbench and his resting place. He often wept and prayed all night.

The sweet rain of the Spirit nourished the seeds sown

in tears by this great pioneer. As the seed bore more fruit, he began to search for more suitable property, which resulted in the purchase of an acre of ground just outside Jewett. On May 25, 1969, Pastor J. Harper Rose snipped a yellow ribbon opening the new building and a new chapter in the history of the church in Harrison County, Ohio.

The history of this assembly is the history of Brother Rose, for the work of the Lord was his life. Always the needs of the church were considered in the family budget. While he never neglected the house of God, Brother Rose was often impatient with his own physical limitations. He always wanted to do more than one day's hours and one man's strength permitted. When he had his tonsils removed, he boarded the train in the morning, underwent surgery at midday, and was home by suppertime. Yet with others in illness, pain, or distress, he was deeply caring and extremely patient.

The saints reflected this spirit of giving. The church at Jewett became known as a giving church, and a large missionary commitment grew ever larger as God blessed. Pastor Rose found a box about the size of an orange crate. This he called the missionary box, and he desired that it literally overflow with offerings for world evangelism. To those with nothing to give, he frequently advised that they look into the box and see the vacant space so that they would "know the need." God rewarded the saints' faithful giving, and in 1973, less than five years after occupancy, the new facility was paid for, and Pastor Rose held a mortgage burning service with great rejoicing. This was one of the last services in which Pastor Rose was able to minister actively. How great was his rejoicing as he led in praises to God for His great blessings!

Pastor Rose preaches the Word.

Pastor Rose with David Willoughby, May 1972.

J. Harper Rose ready to go.

21

JESSE F. SOLOMON

by LaJoyce Martin

To many people, he was the smiling "candy man." He spent 14,400 hours going 250,000 miles to sell $60,761.33 worth of peanut brittle! Every penny of the money went into the church treasury to establish a church in Waco, Texas.

To others, he was a pleasing radio voice. Station KWFT reached from Texas to Oklahoma, Arkansas, Louisiana, Colorado, Kansas, and Nebraska. "The Gospel Church of the Air" became a daily feature. His radio ministry included KSKY (Dallas), KWBU (Corpus Christi), and KFYO (Lubbock).

To some, he was words on a printed page. While pastoring Wichita Falls, he published *The Gospel News* monthly.

But to those of us who knew him personally, he was the soft-spoken, kind-hearted gentleman—accused of being a "softie"—who stood his ground firmly when challenged by trinitarian doctors of divinity and who let the Word work.

Born on July 19, 1909, near Anadarko, Oklahoma,

Jesse F. Solomon gave his life to God early. When he received the Holy Ghost at seventeen, he felt a definite call to preach. There were no Bible schools and few Pentecostal churches. Picture this penniless, frustrated young man, now in his twenties, standing between jerking freight train boxcars. But God thrust him in the ordained direction of victory.

He felt the call to "Go West, young man" so strongly that he left his wife and baby with her mother in Dallas and went to Lamesa, Texas—a small, windblown town in West Texas. Brother Solomon's older brother, who lived northwest of Lamesa, first responded to the Pentecostal truths. Newlyweds Joe and Ruth Blackstock opened their home for prayer meetings and preaching. Others had services in their homes and in the Mungerville school-house. The Lord began to bless and Brother Solomon, along with Joe Blackstock, returned to Dallas in a truck for Brother Solomon's wife, Ollie, and his baby daughter, Christine.

Thirty miles south of Lamesa lay a tiny town called Tarzan. Various churches—Baptist, Church of Christ, Methodist—took turns preaching at the school on Sundays. The Pentecostals had one Sunday a month. Brother Blackstock took the group in his truck and they spent the day.

God began to bless! Joined by W. H. Lyons, Brother Solomon conducted two revivals. Thirty were baptized and twenty received the Holy Ghost. The Solomon's second daughter, Ada Mae, was born in Tarzan.

But the Lord pulled the reins again, this time leading them to Odessa, Texas. Brother Solomon began an ope-nair revival a short block from the main street. He utilized the long front porch of a vacant house for a rostrum, placing seats out front. Great crowds flocked to this meeting. Cars jammed the front and lined up for several blocks around. A cowboy led the Holy Ghost roundup. Brother Callis worked on a ranch near Odessa, and he and his wife ran to the altar and were both filled with the Spirit. This began the First Pentecostal Church of Odessa.

Sister Solomon received the Holy Spirit, and Brother Solomon baptized her in Jesus' name. Their third child, Jerry, was born in nearby Pioneer. A small building housed the first congregation in 1937 under Brother Solomon's leadership.

A neighboring town about the same size, Wink, needed the gospel. For five dollars a month they rented a store. One room in the back was the Solomons' living quarters. Fire gutted a theater, so they obtained the blackened seats and cleaned them up. By spring Sunday school reached seventy.

Wink needed a revival. Steve Odum was contacted but delayed for a week, so Brother Solomon started by himself. By the time the evangelist arrived, the revival blazes burned brightly. About thirty were baptized and twenty received the Spirit. Out on a lease sat a pump house destined to be a church. They purchased it and moved it along with a small donated building that became the parsonage.

The Lord still beckoned westward, but like Jonah, Brother Solomon went another way. After a few months of reverses, he obeyed the call to Hobbs, New Mexico.

A four-week tent revival left ten people wanting to be baptized. Brother Solomon drove about the area looking for water, espying a ranch house with an earthen tank (reservoir) by a windmill. An ideal place! He asked permission to use the tank. The owner quickly agreed—before asking what church. When he found out, he ran into the house, got his Bible, and began to refute baptism in Jesus' name. Brother Solomon took the man's Bible and read the truth to him. Angrily the man asked Brother Solomon to meet his elder. The preacher came over late that evening. It was the same man who had earlier challenged Brother Solomon to a debate! Brother Solomon accepted and, helped by the Lord, expounded the Word for a whole week. But they had to find another place to baptize!

In one year they had a debt-free church and parsonage. Later A. H. Browning built a brick church.

After the assignment in the west was completed in 1939, the Solomon family moved to Rising Star, Texas, to put the children in school while Brother Solomon evangelized. That winter he preached for V. A. Guidroz at Pelly, now known as Baytown. Then he went on to the church pastored by O. F. Fauss.

While he was there tragedy struck at home. While playing two-year-old Floyd Daniel was burned. The Lord forewarned Brother Solomon in a dream and he started home Monday. The child only lived a short time.

Sorely tempted to give up the ministry, the Solomons reconsecrated and sought God's will, preaching here and there. In many towns he was the first to preach the Oneness message.

Pastorates in Lubbock, Wichita Falls, and Dallas followed and a son, David Jesse, arrived. In Dallas, Darlene Marie was born. After evangelizing with a trailer in West Texas and New Mexico, the Solomons took Eldridge Lewis's church in Corpus Christi after his tragic death in an explosion.

Upon request, Brother Solomon became president and business manager of Southern Bible School at Milford, Texas, founded by the L. C. Reeds. The board had voted to close the school, and Brother Solomon spent a year overseeing the closing.

Later this special family went to Waco, Texas, and took Brother Defee's church at 202 Bosque Street. While pastoring the church, Brother Solomon started new works in Corsicana and Marlin. They bought a Methodist church at 1601 Clay Avenue as well as a home. Donna Paulette, the last of the Solomon children, joined the team.

Spliced in between 1950 and 1956 were other pastorates and home missionary efforts that included Fort Worth; McLeod, Texas; Citrus Heights, California; and McGregor, Texas. But Waco was home, and the district board gave Brother Solomon permission to build a new work in north Waco, where he pastored for twenty-two years. This made the seventeenth church he had founded.

In 1959 the building burned, destroying everything. Discouraged, Brother Solomon became ill, requiring hospitalization. The flock scattered, but God was not asleep. Something good was about to happen! First the testing, then the blessing.

An unused church complete with seats, organ, piano, Sunday school rooms, kitchen, dining room, baptistry, and an air conditioner caught Brother Solomon's attention. The trustees of the building gave Brother Solomon permission to use everything free with an option to buy within a year. When the year was up, Brother Solomon offered the people fifteen thousand dollars for the property and they accepted. The Sunday school reached an average of 250 to 300.

The church outgrew their facilities. About four blocks down the street sat a much larger church for sale. The auditorium would seat 450, with two upstairs Sunday school rooms and a fifty-by-sixty-foot annex at the back. It also had a kitchen and a fellowship hall, all air-conditioned. Next to the church sat a three-bedroom brick parsonage and next to that a two-bedroom frame building with almost a block of paved parking area. They bought everything for four hundred dollars a month, and when Brother Solomon resigned in November 1977, the church only owed twenty-seven thousand dollars of the original price of seventy-five thousand dollars.

Two great families contributed much to the growth of the north Waco church—the Johnny Bensons and the Robert Daywitts. Other assistants were the Lindsay Longs and the Regie Francises. For more than two years, H. F. Wilkins was associate pastor. Each pastor had been preaching for fifty years, so they put their "time sheets" together and celebrated "One Hundred Years of Pentecostal Ministry" with a mighty week of teaching and preaching.

On October 8, 1977, the Solomons celebrated their golden wedding anniversary with gifts, best wishes, and money from friends and relatives all across the country. They rejoiced over their seven children, the establishing of seventeen churches, radio programs over fourteen stations, and pastoring twenty churches. It was a memorable celebration! Five days later, on October 13, Sister Ollie Bessie Solomon, a faithful wife and mother, passed away.

Brother Solomon's colorful ministry included serving as state Sunday school director of Texas (1936-38) and superintendent of the North Texas and Panhandle area in the Pentecostal Assemblies of Jesus Christ. He served in the latter capacity from 1940 until the merger that formed the United Pentecostal Church. After the merger, Brother Solomon was the first home missions secretary for Texas. He also served for twenty years on the Texas District Board.

Later Brother Solomon married the former Mrs. Ruth Blackstock, a faithful companion until his death on May 20, 1986. Assisting at the victorious funeral services of this gallant soldier were Brothers W. H. Dean, J. D. Drain, Billy Moore, Paul Hosch, and Laurance Blackstock. From the eulogy of his stepson, Brother Blackstock, we glean the following summary:

"And so that's the way an obituary goes. It gives the birth and the death of a man. But obituaries can never sum up the total of a man's life. It can't give the details of Floyd Solomon's life. It cannot sum up the lifetime of loving, caring, laughing, giving—the joys, tears, and sorrows; it cannot put all of the emotions of seventy-six years into just a few minutes.

"Death has its limitations; there are some things death cannot do. Death cannot rob you of memory. I remember years ago he preached a funeral for a family member that had not lived in the fear of God. I wondered how Brother Solomon was going to approach the service. He said something like this: 'I've never seen a man so bad but there were some good things to say about him, and I've never seen a man so good that there were not some bad things you could say about him.' So death is limited; it cannot rob you of treasured moments.

"Also death cannot rob you of the power of love. The Bible says that many waters cannot quench love, and neither can floods drown it. At the cemetery today we will bury the remains of a body, but we will not bury one ounce of love. All the love that we had yesterday, we still have today.

"Death is further limited in that it cannot destroy hope. We do have a hope beyond the dark veil of death that we will meet again—we will embrace upon the other shore.

"So thank you, Brother Solomon, for blazing the trail before us and showing us how to live life in a good, rich, and beautiful way, for living in such a way that we can have hope in your experience, for the hope that we will meet you again around the throne of Jesus Christ."

Jesse F. Solomon

Golden anniversary.

22

MILFORD STAIRS

by Joyce Morehouse

A hard-working man, Judson Stairs bought and cleared land in the little community of West Waterville, New Brunswick. He was still working on it in 1895 when, on September 30, a fourth baby was born into the family. The family had three boys: Ernest, Burns, and Hughie; and four girls: Ida, Ruby, Rose, and Alma. They named this fourth son Milford.

As a youth Milford volunteered for service in World War I. He boarded the ship *Missinabbi.* As they pulled away from their native soil, Milford went up on the top deck to watch the waves break over the side. A great wave of seasickness overtook him. It was not enough, however, to thwart the young man's enthusiasm for total involvement. They sailed to England and on October 13 went to Shorn Cliffe for training drill until January 1.

From there, Milford was sent across the English Channel to Morel, just behind Vimy Ridge. He was with the Third Ammunition Column and for a while he shoed horses. While he waited for a transfer to the Third Division, he was sent to the First Ammunition Column. There he delivered ammunition to those in the front lines of battle. Finally, he got a transfer to the Thirty-First Battery.

With the Thirty-First Battery Milford found himself in the midst of the fray, fighting in such battles as Passiondale, Amiens Drive, and Vimy Ridge. On August 8, as a volunteer, he made a trip over the top with the Princess Pat Battalion.

On November 11, 1918, the armistice was signed, but the outstanding event in Milford's mind was that on November 10, he was in no man's land under German fire. After the signing of the armistice, he went to Scotland on leave and sailed from there back home to Saint John, first landing in Quebec after a thirteen-day sea passage.

While serving his country, Milford won a number of medals as well as a letter of commendation from King George V. He was discharged from service on May 14, 1919.

After returning from overseas, Milford came to the Lord when Brother John Dearing brought the message of Jesus Name baptism to New Brunswick. He baptized several people including Edgar Grant, Leonard Parent, and Milford, Wynn, and Quincy Stairs. In 1922, Milford was ordained into the ministry.

In 1924 Milford assisted in tent meetings, along with several other young ministers. They pitched a tent on Woodstock Road and first introduced Pentecost to Fredericton. One of the brethren later recalled that "Milford would get excited and start quoting Scripture as loudly as he could, and the more excited he became, the louder he yelled."

In July 1929 Milford had a flat tire as he drove through Clarendon, New Brunswick. He went into a nearby store and asked, "Can someone take me to the next village to get a tire?" The proprietor of the store, Noble Johnston, consented to do so, then invited his daughter, Marguerite, to go along with them. She declined, but later her mother invited Milford in and introduced him to Marguerite. They learned that he was holding special meetings nearby, so Marguerite went to hear him preach. The following year on June 29, 1930, Maggie Johnston became Milford Stairs's bride.

At this time Milford pastored at Millville, so Maggie joined him there. The people loved their pastor and his new wife. A great worker, Brother Stairs soon managed to move from the hall where they held services and build a new church. They also had their own home in Millville, but just as they were getting established, their new home burned. Their first child, Carol, was born here. (Today Carol lives in Baton Rouge, Louisiana.)

Brother Stairs had a most unusual and peculiar characteristic. When he would pray for someone's healing, people could be sure his faith had touched God and the work was done when he started whistling in the Spirit.

When the Stairs family left Millville, they went to a relatively new work in Ripples, a small community where God had reached out to save several people. While the Stairses were in Ripples, their baby boy was born, but he only lived a few days. Because Brother Stairs had longed for a son, he was almost beside himself with grief. He went into the little church in Ripples, and God miraculously visited him in his sorrow and restored his spirit.

He spent many hours working on the parsonage and building the church in the community and won the respect of all who knew him. A tremendous student of the

Word, he was my first pastor, as my parents had only recently been saved and were totally reliant on the teaching of this man of God.

Brother Stairs started the work at Houlton, Maine, and at Montecello he baptized twenty-four from a trinitarian assembly, along with their two leaders, in Jesus' name. Milford evangelized frequently, while his wife took care of the church. He preached in such places as Stickney, Millville, Sussex, Ripples, and Doaktown. They pastored in Chipman, Prince Edward Island, and on the Miramichi. Their youngest daughter, Sharon, was born in Doaktown.

For a number of years Milford worked beside his wife at the United Pentecostal Bible Institute in Marysville, where she held numerous positions. They first went there following the opening in 1955 and also started and pastored the Marysville church. They liked the place so well that Milford finally built a home on the banks of the Nashwaak River, with a big picture window overlooking the stream. Brother Stairs continued to attend service at times, although he was hospitalized off and on. He maintained a reasonable state of health for his age, and he turned ninety on September 30, 1985.

God surely blessed this faithful pioneer of the gospel and has doubly blessed those who have come to know the spirit of this fine man of God. He was a true soldier—a soldier of the cross for his God.

Editor's note: Milford Stairs laid down his cross and the sword of the Lord on January 1, 1990.

Rev. and Mrs. Milford Stairs on his 90th birthday.

Bro. and Sis. M. Stairs, Carol and Grenville Evans and Sharon in the early 1950s.

Bro. Stairs baptizing in Jesus' name, 1951.

Hebert Starr

23

HEBERT STARR

by Philip S. Cornell

No man was prouder to be a Hoosier than Hebert Starr. Although he has spent the majority of his adult life in the state of Michigan and transplanted his immediate family here, he has never forgotten his roots. He was born on the farm that belonged to the Starr family for several generations before his birth. This farm is located on a ridge overlooking Bartlettsville, Indiana, a small village near Bedford. The ridge has often been called Starr Ridge. Several of Hebert Starr's relatives still live along that ridge.

Hebert Starr was born on May 5, 1900, as the second son of Oscar and Charlotte Ross Starr. His father was generally considered to be a good man who led a peaceful life and went to church occasionally. He was also a fiercely independent man. His mother also had the reputation of being an honest and straightforward woman who led a clean life and tried to teach her children to do the same. Hebert had four brothers: Lebert, Noble, Jesse, and Gerald.

Most of Hebert's memories of childhood are pleasant.

Hebert remembers evenings spent with his own family or visiting his uncle's family or his grandparents, who lived nearby. This bonding, or sense of family, was one of the more important things that Hebert Starr was able to pass on. Among his fondest memories are his early days on the farm.

He attended a one-room schoolhouse. Hebert was good at arithmetic and spelling, but not as good at reading. This he later felt was because he was nearsighted, and during that time very few people owned glasses.

One of the best remembered events of Hebert's childhood occurred in 1910 when he and his brothers first saw the bright red roadster of Dr. Worley, the Starr family physician. When Dr. Worley finished his visit and was about to leave, he must have seen the earnest, pleading look on the boys' faces, because he offered them a ride to Bartlettsville. He told them, however, that they would have to walk home. They were so delighted at the chance to ride in the automobile, they quickly accepted.

In 1918, Hebert obtained his first job away from home. He was hired by a railroad "extra gang" in Terre Haute, Indiana. He stayed in a small hotel in Terre Haute where the food was provided as part of the lodging fee.

In Bedford, Indiana, a position opened up in the sawmill. The family sawmill on the farm aided him in obtaining this employment.

Although he owned a horse and buggy, they were no match for the new technology, at least insofar as attracting members of the opposite sex. Hebert soon felt that he had to have his own car. He worked hard in the sawmill and lived simply and frugally for the next two years to save as much money as he possibly could.

During this period of time he met Eleanor Hudson from Heltonville, Indiana, a dark-haired, beautiful young woman. On their first date, he took her to a picnic in his horse and buggy. Thereafter, for a considerable period of time, Hebert lost track of Eleanor.

In 1922, Hebert purchased his own new automobile. Soon thereafter, he had another date with Eleanor Hudson. During the next several weeks, they were together often. Eleanor was bright and spontaneous and tried to (if not insisted on) enjoy life in the present. Hebert was more cautious and deliberate, with certain long-term goals. This conflict of personalities and aspirations would cause some difficulty, but in many ways it brought out the best in both Hebert and Eleanor.

Hebert recalls the time he asked Eleanor to marry him. They were driving his horse and buggy near the Todd farm, which he had managed a few years earlier. They came upon an outdoor meeting of the Ku Klux Klan. Fearful, Eleanor begged, "Hebert, take me away from here right now!" Hebert sensed his opportunity and interjected, "Eleanor, if you will marry me, I will protect you from the Klan and anyone else." Eleanor, apparently anxious and sensing the possibility of a greater danger, quickly accepted the offer.

Eleanor, now deceased, recalled the commitment to marriage in a somewhat different light. She remembered that on their wedding day, March 3, 1923, they went to the justice of the peace at the square in Bedford. Hebert became indecisive. Apparently, he commenced to walk with her around the square several times. Eleanor, sensing that Hebert might be getting cold feet, informed him that if they walked around the square again, she would not marry him. Hebert stopped and went to the justice of the peace and they were married.

Hebert worked for the Shea Donley Stone Company and became a skilled planer. About this time his eldest son, William Richard, was born. This was a very happy event in Hebert and Eleanor's lives, a time when Hebert's goals in life were solidified. He cut stone for numerous buildings, many of which are in Washington, D. C., Pittsburgh, Pennsylvania, and other metropolitan areas.

During the 1920s and until the Great Depression, the economy was good and the work was steady at the stone quarry. Although the stock market crashed in 1929, it was not until 1932 that the stone quarry shut down for long periods of time. Suddenly Hebert was without a job. He had no control over his life and that of his family. He was willing to work but could not. He even sold apples. Life became desperate, with hardly enough money for food, let alone house payments and entertainment.

Eleanor enjoyed life and especially entertainment. She often insisted that Hebert take her to shows in and around the Bedford area. Now there was no money for such entertainment. Eleanor heard about a little church on Fourteenth Street where the Pentecostals met together for worship services. "I hear they put on quite a show. They say sometimes the ministers or even other people dance down the aisles," she said. "And they tell me that the music is lively and entertaining. Best of all, this performance costs nothing." She soon talked Hebert into going to a service.

Thereafter, they commenced going to several services with their family. They both felt convicted of sins and felt a need for God in their lives. The church they were going to was commonly referred to as the One God Pentecostal Church, located near the city dump in downtown Bedford on Fourteenth Street, pastored by Reverend C. J. Davis.

Hebert considers the night he received the Holy Ghost to be the single most important event in his life. The evangelist was J. L. Patton. Hebert had felt conviction at other services but had not responded to the altar calls. He and Eleanor had discussed this at home and had talked about what it would mean to live as Christians. Often, Eleanor suggested that the next time Hebert was in church and felt the call of God he should go to the altar; however, Hebert was still reluctant. But soon he found the courage to respond to the altar call.

At the moment he made a move toward the altar, Eleanor had second thoughts. Later she confessed that she was hopeful of continuing the lifestyle that they had before and did not want to become connected with these Pentecostal people. So she moved to stop Hebert's progress toward the altar, grabbing hold of him to prevent him from going to the altar. Her hands grasped the jacket that he was wearing and held fast. He slipped out of the coat and went straight to the altar.

Prior to that time, Hebert had developed a habit of smoking cigarettes. Although this was long before present.-day warnings of the physical dangers of smoking, smoking was thought of as a rather dirty habit. Shortly after attending the church, he picked up a cigarette and lit it. He immediately felt a deadening sensation starting at the top of his head and working down through his body. Frightened, he thought he might be having a stroke or even be dying. He prayed, promising God that if that feeling were taken from him, he would never smoke again. He put out the cigarette. Then the deadening feeling lifted. A short time later, apparently dubious that he had received such a signal from God, Hebert started to smoke another cigarette. Again, the deadening feeling came, and again, he prayed and promised never to smoke again. This second time convinced this Hoosier that he should never smoke again. He has not since that day. It was a few nights later that he was filled with the Holy Ghost.

All was not bliss, however, in the Starr household. Eleanor had not yet joined Hebert in the church. Initially, she was very upset by his conversion to Pentecost. She had only intended to go there to see the show. She resisted the change in his life and often discussed and debated the matter with him. She did, however, continue to attend church with him. Before long she also followed her husband into the church.

Economically, things did not change for the better for the Starr family. Almost everyone was out of work at that time, and there was little prospect for jobs in Bedford. Hebert and Eleanor now had other children: daughters Gloria, Oweetah, and Phyllis, and son H. James.

Although this was a tough time economically, Hebert grew spiritually. He was beginning to feel his call of God to the ministry. He spent much of his spare time in the study of the Bible and in discussions with his wife and son William, trying to learn as much as he could as fast as he could. Many passages of Scripture opened up to him in a way that they never had before. His Bible became his constant companion. He read and reread certain passages of Scripture, each time getting something new and beneficial. He had never realized before what a wonderful book the Bible was. Eleanor and William experienced the same sort of growth in their spiritual lives. Hebert first became a lay minister in the local church in Bedford, and prior to moving to Michigan, he became the assistant pastor.

The family moved to Lansing in 1938. Hebert found work through the use of his old trade, cutting stone, with the Roy Beard Cutstone Company in Lansing. Work became unsteady. Hebert sought whatever odd jobs he could. He finally found work shoveling snow outside the Fisher Body plant. Thereafter, he was hired by the Oldsmobile Division of General Motors as a plant worker. He worked there for the next twenty years while he built the church and raised his family.

The first church in Lansing was located at 131 South Hosmer. The family lived in this house also.

During this time Hebert learned that a truck driver had a lot for sale at 601 South Francis. He offered it to Hebert for ten dollars plus Hebert's promise to pay the back taxes. Hebert purchased the lot and began digging a basement for a church. The conditions were less than ideal. Much of the work was done by hand during the winter months, and Michigan has cold winters. Hebert and his son William did most of the unbelievably hard work. Any help that was given was looked upon as proof positive that God answered prayers. After work, Hebert would board the bus each day from their home on Beach Street to go to the church site to work well into the evening. Many of the churches that formed the core of the initial work in the state of Michigan also helped.

Soon thereafter, Hebert found a lot located at 522 South Francis, about half a block away from the church. Here he built his second home. Again he received help from several men in the churches located in other cities.

He and Eleanor were to live at this address for most of the years that they pastored in Lansing.

This church is one of the pioneer churches of the Michigan District United Pentecostal Church. Over the years, hundreds, if not thousands, of people received an introduction to Pentecost. An untold amount of ministers, especially from the Midwest, have at one time or another preached at the church located at 601 South Francis. During the course of his ministry, Hebert Starr baptized over six hundred people, most of whom received the Holy Spirit. He and Eleanor worked diligently to make sure that the work in Lansing progressed.

Their home was always an open home in which one could come and feel welcome. Anyone associated with the church work was treated as a close friend and almost a family member. Most visitors quickly sensed the commitment, integrity, and friendship that was so much a part of the family. Their lives centered around the church work— the most important thing in their lives.

Hebert enjoyed his family. Eleanor and Hebert considered the lives of their children to be very important and interacted with them wherever and whenever possible. Both Hebert and Eleanor were interested in their children obtaining good education. At times, their children would bring home friends from school, and they were readily accepted into the Starr home. Very often a conversation would ensue between these school friends and Hebert and Eleanor. Lively conversations would take place on various subjects, but more often than not, at one time or another, they turned towards church work and salvation.

Hebert and Eleanor were also committed to people in

need. The members of their church in Lansing came from all walks of life. Several came from different ethnic and racial backgrounds. Most, if not all, could have been classified as poor. Both Hebert and Eleanor felt a strong obligation to attend to the needs of these people and minister to them. If Hebert or Eleanor knew of it, no church member ever went without a basic necessity of life.

Hebert Starr valued children. For the better part of two generations he has given candy to children at the conclusion of most services. People who have reflected upon their childhood interactions with Hebert recall them as fond memories.

Toward the end of his pastorship of the Lansing church, Hebert purchased some lots on the south side of Lansing on the corner of Jolly Road and Starr Avenue as a place for a new church. He saw to it that the lots were properly rezoned before resigning. In 1971, Hebert Starr resigned as the pastor of the East Side Apostolic Tabernacle in Lansing, Michigan, and turned the work over to his grandson, David D. Stephens.

Brother Stephens was able to build a new church on the lots. Life Christian Church building is overflowing. A new church on M-99 near I-96 has the first wing completed. In recent years, the church has established a private Christian school and child care center at the church.

Hebert Starr's oldest son, William R. Starr, was the district superintendent for the Michigan District United Pentecostal Church from 1958 until his death in 1987. He took over a prayer meeting group in Albion, Michigan. This church in Albion is one of the prominent churches of that community and one of the most successful in the Michigan District.

Douglas Stephens, Hebert's son-in-law, also came out of the church in Lansing. In 1954, he started the United Pentecostal Church in Owosso. In 1963, he began a work in Grand Ledge and has, at the present time, a very successful church. He was formerly Pentecostal Conqueror's president and secretary for the Michigan District for about fifteen years. He has, at various times since, been a member of the Michigan Board for almost twenty years. His wife, Gloria, a daughter of Hebert's, was the editor of the *Michigan District News* since its inception in 1956, serving as editor for thirty-four years.

Another daughter of Hebert's, Phyllis Cornell, is a member of the First United Pentecostal Church of Grand Ledge, Michigan. She has served for twelve years as the circulation manager for the *Michigan District News*. For approximately twenty years she was the head cook at the Michigan District Camp during the family camp sessions and was also the conference cook.

Hebert's youngest son, H. James Starr, is a prominent and respected attorney practicing in Lansing, Michigan.

Several of Hebert Starr's grandchildren are involved in United Pentecostal churches in various parts of the United States.

In retirement, Hebert Starr has continued to travel widely throughout the United States. He is especially fond of returning to Paul Jordan's church in Indianapolis, Indiana. Brother Jordan has always been kind and considerate of Hebert Starr and is among his closest friends. In September of 1977, Hebert lost his beloved wife, Eleanor. She had been his friend, confidante, and advisor in life. The death of Eleanor was a most significant loss for Hebert. She had been his mate for the entire period of his adulthood. He trusted her. Even though they did not always agree, he knew that Eleanor's opinions were sincerely held. He always felt that she looked out for what she believed was his best interest. She was his constant companion. Very often, when the world around him threatened, he was still able to talk it over with Eleanor. He understood that she had a keen and clever mind, and admired her for it. In many ways, she gave him the self-confidence necessary to achieve some of the important things he did in life.

Hebert lived in an apartment provided by the Christ Apostolic Church in Albion, Michigan. His son William, the pastor of the church, and William's wife, June, supported and maintained him for ten years. Then he moved to a senior citizen complex in Lansing.

In reflecting upon his life, Hebert believes that his salvation is the greatest thing that ever happened to him. He says, "It gave me a happy life." He believes that it replaced a probable failure with a success both here on earth and after death in heaven. He says that salvation helps one to get along and that "God works things ultimately to your favor."

Accomplishments mean more when a person bases his actions on something other than getting ahead in this life. Doing so also minimizes the potential for conflict with others. His advice to young ministers is to "love God, love the people of God and, in fact, all people." He believes that it is absolutely important to keep God's commandments. He also believes it is important to be humble, regardless of a person's station in this life. "Make as many friends as you can, and whenever you have the opportunity, help someone in need. Do not stand in the way of success of others."

Hebert has twenty-three grandchildren and nineteen great-grandchildren. Most of them are involved in one way or another in the church. Along with his wife, Eleanor, he has also lost in this life his daughter Oweetah in 1985, and his son William in 1987.

United Pentecostal Church, 2045 W. Jolly Road, Lansing, Michigan Hebert Starr pastor emeritus.

24

WILLIAM R. STARR

by Marion June Starr

William Richard Starr was born September 16, 1924, in Bedford, Indiana, to Hebert and Eleanor Starr. He was the firstborn. Following him were Gloria, Oweetah, Phyllis, and James. Eleanor had a very difficult birth with William and thought she would die. Then and there she dedicated him to God. Even though she wasn't a Christian at the time, she was aware of God.

When Billy (as he was called then) was two years old, he was kicked in the mouth by a mule at his grandfather's farm. His gums and teeth were torn loose from his mouth. Hebert and Eleanor were frantic. Eleanor remembered her brother M. M. Hudson, who attended Brother Rowe's church in Mishawaka, Indiana, and had been baptized in Jesus' name by G. T. Haywood. He had witnessed to them many times but they weren't interested. Desperately they called for him to pray for Billy. God healed Bill so completely that a specialist who examined him asked them why they had called him. This miracle of healing opened their eyes to the power of God.

In 1932 Bill was baptized and filled with the Holy

Ghost, along with his parents, during J. L. Patton's revival at Pastor James Davis's church in Bedford, Indiana. A fervent little boy, William testified anointedly at an early age. He still seemed to get involved in a few fights, however. One day when his mother drove to pick him up from school, she had a slight accident while watching some boys fighting, thinking Billy was one of them. Many years later a minister reminded Billy that when he saw him go to the altar he knew that he had been in another fight.

In 1938 the Starrs moved to Lansing, Michigan, and started a church in their house. In 1940 they started construction of a church on Francis Street. Bill was sixteen. He came home from high school many nights and helped make cement with salt added to keep it from freezing. He dreamed of digging and digging in the frozen ground. He said his father taught him one thing—not to build in the winter.

Bill was the only saved young person in the high school he attended. He took education very seriously and felt that an Apostolic should be the best representative possible. He was on the debate team in high school and later helped his coach, T. J. Harris, coach other students.

After he completed high school, he enrolled at Michigan State University. He was youth leader for a fellowship during this time. During his first semester World War II began and he was drafted at eighteen. He served three years in the Air Force. Having been healed of asthma, he was able to fly at a high altitude. He was a radio operator. During one of his missions the plane was hit by flak, knocking off his oxygen hose. The pilot heard him mumble and told someone to see about the preacher. They thought he was gone. As soon as his hose was smacked in place, he started talking as if nothing had happened. God had saved his life.

In November 1945, after having been discharged from the army, he decided to travel. He went with his uncle M. M. Hudson to a convention at Christian Tabernacle in Indianapolis, Indiana, where Lena Spillman was pastor. I met Bill for the first time when he and Brother Hudson visited my father's church during the convention. It was just a casual meeting, and he seemed very shy. Bill went back to Ann Arbor, Michigan, and enrolled at the University of Michigan to continue his education that had been interrupted by the war.

Brother and Sister Anderson moved from Indianapolis to Jackson, Michigan, and began to pastor the group turned over to them by Brother Hudson. They asked me to move to Jackson to play their music. In August 1946 I married Bill. We moved to Ypsilanti and lived in housing for married couples going to school. We had very little, but I was thrilled with that little three-room apartment. Bill's mother had collected odds and ends of furniture for us. We used crate boxes to store our many books. I had never used a wood-burning cookstove in my life. I used some soft coal and smoked up the house. I turned to hot plates after that!

Bill was a brilliant man but seemed to have little mechanical expertise—or at least very little interest. He decided to paint our living room while I was away. Thinking he knew what he was doing, I chose a lovely rose color. He borrowed someone's spray gun, thinking that it would be faster. When I came home, I found rose-colored furniture, and I could trace the irregular path of the spray gun as it went over the walls in deep and light paths. We laughed about the state of things, but I determined then and there that I would take care of the painting after that.

His mind had a tendency to be preoccupied when working with his hands. He would often proudly tell about his wife and her toolbox. He allowed me a free hand in the house. I could tear down walls, paint, or do whatever I wanted to in the house. He would praise the finished work but wanted no part of the construction. I enjoyed the planning and redoing.

In July 1947 Marcia June Starr was born.

Bill received his Bachelor's degree in 1948 and his Master's degree in 1949, majoring in history. He studied Greek and Hebrew.

He had plans for building a church in Chicago or some other large city. After graduation we moved to Lansing to attend his father's church until he could decide where to go. Due to a recession at this time, he had little success in finding the type of employment he wanted. He decided to take a civil service test to work for the secretary of state as a driver's license administrator for several counties. He got the position, and we moved to Coldwater. He was to be in this position for the next twenty-five years.

Brother Gus Anderson asked us to take a little group in Albion, Michigan, that held services in the hall of the Veterans of Foreign Wars. In the month of June 1951 my husband was voted in as pastor by three people. We organized a Sunday school with an attendance of seven people that first Sunday. Our Sunday school increased each week, with many coming from the surrounding countryside as well as the city.

In October 1952, Alexa Renee Starr was born. We

were happy in the work of God and with our little family. We began to feel a great need for our own church building. In 1954 we purchased property on Lincoln and Adams streets. We dug the basement, covered it over, and held services there. When it rained, the flat roof allowed the rain to come through in several places. We swept and mopped water and repaired the roof on a regular basis.

God blessed, however, and sent in new souls. Many were young couples like us, and we had an abundance of children who are the backbone of the church today. Some of the many ministers who preached there were Brother and Sister Anton Huba, M. M. Hudson, Gus Anderson, Donnie Winters, Ernest Jolly, W. K. Carouthers, Howard Goss, Albert Abbey, and a host of others.

There were many healings. Ernest Shaffer's father was healed of a cancer on his head when he got baptized in Jesus' name. Phyllis and Paul Woods' daughter, Wendi, was healed of a large tumor on her back and is still healed today. Dolly Young was given up to die with cancer and was even in a semi-coma when God healed her, and she is still living today.

Brother Starr served as youth president of the United Pentecostal Church from 1950 to 1954. He then served as presbyter until 1959. He was elected district superintendent at the age of thirty-four. He was young, but wise beyond his years.

Rebecca Jean Starr was born in October 1955. In November 1957, Priscilla Eleanor was born. Bill was very busy. He still worked for the state, was district superintendent, and pastored. On his way to work in the morning he would drop the girls off at school. This was the time he used for quizzing them about their grades and admonishing

247

them to look straight at the teacher. Every morning before the girls left for school we prayed with them and asked God to protect their minds.

When the girls were old enough to date, he gave them money. He told them to buy their own hamburger or take a taxi home if the boy did not behave himself. He also told them not to order too much in a restaurant because the boy might not have much money.

He loved his girls and was interested in every part of their lives. When they were married and were pastors' wives, he would wait Sunday night after church for their calls to find out how many got saved and how many were in Sunday school. His usual question was, "Have the girls checked in?" He was a loving husband, romantic, and very respectful of my opinion.

Sometimes he liked to play jokes on the girls. We had a screened-in area at the back of our house. One evening Alexa was reading with the light on. She came into the kitchen for something and left her book. In the meantime Bill slipped down, unscrewed the light bulb, and sat in her chair. Alexa went back and tried the light, wondering why it would not turn on. She gave up and reached for her book in the dark. When she did she touched a human hand. She let out a bloodcurdling scream, and her dad burst into laughter.

In February 1965 another little girl, Sara Lee, was added to the four girls. In the fall of 1965 Marcia married a young evangelist, Martyn Ballestero.

This was also the year that the district made plans to build a campground, probably one of the greatest stresses in our life. The contractors went bankrupt, and businesses began slapping liens against the camp. The district voted to raise more money to save our camp, which had approximately one hundred acres with a mile of streets and sewers. There are seventy modern cottages, an air-conditioned dining room, educational buildings, and the William R. Starr Tabernacle, where services are held throughout most of the summer.

Brother Starr was also the driving force behind the Apostolic Institute of Development, a summer Bible course for those who wanted an accelerated course of study. Brothers Mooney, Nix, Grisham, Henson, and Deeds taught various subjects, and Brother Starr taught doctrinal subjects. These brothers along with Brother Starr wrote a huge textbook.

Brother Starr's sisters, Gloria Stephens and Phyllis Cornell, along with their husbands, work tirelessly for the camp, scouting out equipment.

Brother Starr served as associate editor of the *Michigan District News* for thirty years, with his sister Gloria Stephens serving as editor for thirty-four years. He was on the General Board for twenty-eight consecutive years. He also served one two-year term as executive presbyter and then another as executive presbyter for the eastern part of the United States. One year he wrote for the Sunday school Division. He served on the Budget Committee as well as on the Judicial Committee. He wrote sermons for the *Albion Journal* and a pamphlet on the Godhead.

Brother Starr was known in the district for his half glasses. He had an unusual way of thrusting his arms straight up when he reached the pulpit and saying, "Praise the Lord!"

My husband was a most articulate speaker. He had a

way with words and could say more with the least words. He had some unusual sayings. One of them was, "I would rather go to bed with a wet, mangy dog than a guilty conscience." Another was, "Don't pay a false doctrine preacher to go to hell. Go free of charge." Brother Starr was a dedicated man of the gospel. He was the happiest when going to church and working in some capacity connected with the church. He was a fiery preacher and usually hit the pulpit preaching. He ended quickly.

Our daughter Alexa was now married to a young preacher, Fredrick Olson, from Texas. In 1973, having need of larger facilities, we purchased a large Baptist church on the main street of town. It was a beautiful church and Brother Starr loved it. In 1974 our daughter Rebecca married evangelist David Trammell, who is now the pastor of Christ Apostolic Church of Albion. Our daughter Priscilla is married to evangelist Curtis Spears, and our youngest, Sara, is married to evangelist Tom Copple. We have fourteen grandchildren: Anthony, Bryan, Martyn, Marisa, and Andrew Ballestero; Aaron and Shauna Olson; Marcus and Farrah Trammell; Brittany, Ashley, Charity, and Natalie Hutchison; and Sharayah Copple. Anthony and Bryan are now preaching. Our grandchildren are fifth-generation Apostolics.

Brother Starr enjoyed his preacher sons-in-law. At Christmas time we had tag-team preaching on the service before Christmas. He called them by number: son-in-law number one, number two, and so on according to age. They all sat on the platform together. The saints enjoyed hearing them. III John 4 describes how we felt about our children: "I have no greater joy than to hear that my children walk in truth."

It was little over a month after a great Christmas with the family that at age sixty-two Brother Starr died suddenly with a massive heart attack. His funeral was held in the large chapel of Albion College. The newspaper said over 1,600 people attended the funeral and that it was one of the largest ever in Albion. Many preachers came from as far as California and Mississippi, and some could not get a flight because of a snowstorm. Our general superintendent, Nathaniel Urshan, flew to Chicago and rented a car to get to the funeral. Many Executive Board members called our home. Sister Helen Cole called me from Australia. The city of Albion banned parking for two blocks around the church for those who went to see Brother Starr lying in state at the church.

Brother Starr's only goal in life was to do as much as possible for God. Everything he did he wanted to count for God. His life made an impact on his own brother and sisters, his nieces and nephews, and our own children and grandchildren. My children quote him, and I find myself constantly referring to something he taught or said. My son-in-law David and daughter Rebecca are carrying on with the church with great spiritual outpouring. Brother Starr loved his saints and would be happy that they are moving on. My daughters and sons-in-law have been a great source of comfort and inspiration.

Brother Starr's great ministry left its mark in the lives he touched. "Henceforth there is laid up for me a crown of righteousness, which the Lord, the righteous judge, shall give me at that day: and not to me only, but unto all them also that love his appearing" (II Timothy 4:8). Amen!

Bill and June Anderson Starr, wedding, August 28, 1946.

Rev. and Mrs. William R. Starr

Christ Apostolic Church, Albion, Michigan, founded by William R. Starr.

Mrs. William R. Starr and family, 1991.

25

L. T. STRONG

by L. T. Strong

I grew up near Jackson in the hills of Tennessee. At eighteen, I was living a life of wasted years in sin. I had stooped so low in sin that God alone knew what I had done. Thank God for His love and tender mercy to me.

One night I walked under an old-fashioned brush arbor where Albert D. Gurley and Newt Graves were preaching this glorious gospel according to Acts 2:38 and Joel 2:27-28. God knocked at my heart's door, but what a sad mistake I made! I listened to the devil and went on in sin as thousands of young people do until it is too late. Praise the Lord, I had a Holy Ghost-filled mother, sisters, and saints praying for me. Brother Guy Webb of Bemis pastored a little church near us.

One night I went to the altar. Miserable and carrying that heavy yoke of sin's bondage, I knelt and repented of my sins. Brother Webb baptized me in the wonderful name of Jesus on the first Sunday in March in 1929. God gloriously filled me with the precious Holy Ghost. Five months later He called me to preach this precious truth.

At the time I started preaching, I was twenty years

old. I traveled by foot with just a few clothes in my suit-case and my Bible in my hand. Sometimes I had blisters on my feet and no money in my pocket, but I had Jesus by my side. Often I stopped along the road, went into the woods, and prayed with a broken heart for a lost world, not knowing where I would lay my head that night.

Jesus said to me, "I am with you always, even unto the end of the world." Even though I am nearing the end of my way, I am not road weary nor discouraged. I am still hungry to tell someone about the wonderful name of Jesus.

In those days I would stop along the highways to wit-ness in honky-tonks, whiskey stores, and beer joints. When I got to a town, I would visit the jails and state pris-ons, witnessing to prisoners, from as few as one to as many as a hundred. I told them how Jesus suffered for them and that He loved them. (See Isaiah 53 and Acts 2:38-39.)

Time after time I left men shedding tears and asking me to return. I have preached this truth when men would lie in wait by the road and try to beat me to death, where they burned brush arbors and churches, broke up revivals, and brought ropes to hang me. The law officers sometimes would even uphold these men in their evil deeds. Little did they realize I was on the Lord's side. Captain Jesus and His host were with us and were much greater than they.

At the age of twenty-five I married a fine Pentecostal girl, Belva Willis, who labored with me in the gospel until the Lord called her from her field of labor on December 23, 1972. God gave us three fine children, two boys and one daughter. Many years ago we went to Florida, where

God gave us a harvest of many souls for our labors.

We established a fine church in Arbundale, Florida, where we pastored for several years. The Lord blessed us in a wonderful way. Johnny Lipham is the present pastor; he is one of the fine young men God brought into the truth under my ministry, along with Billy Cupples, who lost his life on the mission field in Africa.

A number of young men whom God called to preach this truth came in during my revivals. Several of them have gone on to their reward. I am so glad that God has let me stay in His harvest field to help gather in the golden grain. I feel like Caleb did when he asked Joshua to give him his inheritance in the mountain among the giants. In the name of Jesus with prayer and faith continually night and day, I can make it.

I have found God's grace is sufficient and that His strength is made perfect in weakness. Jesus prepared me a table in the presence of my enemies. (See Psalm 23:5.) While they were starving to death, my soul was like a stall-fed calf. The apostle Paul wrote, "All that will live godly in Christ Jesus shall suffer persecution" (II Timothy 3:12). I am not worrying about the reward that I will receive at the end of life's journey; my greatest concern is finishing the work that Jesus has given me to do before He catches the church away.

Five years ago this May, I was stricken with cancer. After two surgeries and forty-five cobalt treatments, I was very sick because I did not respond to the treatment. While I was in the hospital for the third operation, the general conference of the United Pentecostal Church International convened in Kansas City. A prayer request was called in for me and the churches in the surrounding area were praying for me. God healed me completely; there is no sign of cancer in my body anymore.

I want to be faithful until I reach the end of my journey. In Hebrews 11, all the elders had a good report. Through faith they made it, even though they did not have what we have. I am persuaded that we can make it too.

If I never meet you on this earth, please do not sell your birthright. Just one step on that street of gold will be worth it all!

L. T. Strong preaches the Word.

26

URBAN T. VANDERHOFF

by Doris Cooke Vanderhoff

As he watched people praying at the altar on his first visit to a Pentecostal church, Urban Vanderhoff found the answer to a question he had asked since childhood. As a child he had heard about Abraham, Isaac, and Jacob, who talked to God. When he asked, "Why don't people talk to God now?" he was told, "People don't talk to God like that anymore." Now he knew differently; these people really talked to God.

Ait Vanderhoff was born in Holland and then lived in Germany before coming to America. Anna Goldenstein and her family came to America from Germany. Apparently they met in America. After they married, they bought a farm in northwest Iowa. Ait and Anna had eight children, five boys and three girls. Urban Theron Vanderhoff, born April 25, 1906, was the fifth child.

When he was a child his family attended the German Lutheran church, but as he grew older they no longer attended. The farm boy worked hard. By age nine he drove a team of horses on a hay stacker and at twelve he took a man's place on the buck rake, bucking hay. Never one to shun work, he climbed ladders and painted houses when he was in his seventies and planted a garden until he was eighty.

In 1924 at eighteen he attended a tent meeting in the small town of Greenville, Iowa. Joe Barnett was conducting services there along with Brother Alison from Des Moines. Here Urban repented of his sins. Brother Anderson, another worker with Brother Barnett, baptized him a week later, and shortly afterwards God filled him with the Holy Ghost in a prayer meeting in his home.

People soon noticed a difference in Urban's life. When he refused a cigarette his brother-in-law said, "I guess you are going to quit smoking and act like those people now." After he received the Holy Ghost, a friend inquired, "Where have you been? I haven't seen you at the dances or anywhere else?" After talking a while this friend suddenly asked, "Say, how did you quit swearing?" Urban recalled, "I honestly didn't know that I swore so much, but my friend immediately detected the change in me."

Earlier his older brother George had married and moved to a farm near Rossie, Iowa. He attended a tent meeting also held by Brother Barnett, and George had been in church for about two years. The family was upset that George put church first, which made him late for family affairs. By 1926 when the church in Spencer, Iowa, was built, George and Urban as well as their parents and the whole family except two married sisters were in the church.

While still on the farm, one of the younger brothers took a loaded manure spreader, pulled by four horses, out into the field. He crawled under the spreader to repair it and it fell on him. His brother ran to the house yelling,

"Theron is dying!" Quickly they jumped into the car and drove across the field to help. The three brothers grabbed hold of the spreader and tried to lift it. It didn't move. One brother said, "We can't lift it; we'll have to try something else." Urban said, "Let's try one more time." As they took hold of the spreader, he prayed, "In the name of Jesus!" They lifted the spreader up with no effort at all. Theron crawled out from under it but was still unable to sit up. When the boys prayed again, Theron got up and walked away. Later the four boys tried to lift the spreader after they emptied it, but they could not budge it.

In 1927 while still attending the church in Spencer, Urban met a young visitor, Doris McKee, who became his wife on March 10, 1928. Their pastor, Oran White, was not yet ordained, so a Baptist minister performed the ceremony. In September 1928, George and Urban and their wives went to Pennsylvania to hold meetings near Erie. This began a life of nearly sixty years in the ministry.

Sister Ruth Kuttcump pastored a church in Rock Island, Illinois, that the two brothers attended briefly. In November 1928, they went to Whitehall, Illinois, and Brother Barnett helped them locate an upstairs hall where George and Urban held nightly meetings until March 1929.

For four months, with no rest nights, the people came in all kinds of weather. They chopped holes in the ice to baptize people in a nearby stream. Many received the Holy Ghost and God blessed with His presence and healing power. That spring Urban and Doris returned to Spencer, but George stayed on at Whitehall as pastor.

For two and a half years Urban and his wife made Spencer their home church under Pastor Cleve Curley.

During this time they held services in various places including Terrell, Iowa, where Grace Cook and Florence Clooney were trying to establish a church. They also held services in the chapel of a funeral home in Worthington, Minnesota, briefly. Their first child, a son named Myrlin, was born in Spencer. In the fall of 1931 they returned to Davenport. While there they assisted Sister Ruth Kuttcump and held services in nearby towns.

During the Depression Urban picked corn for one and a half cents a bushel. At one place everyone had a small garden and they all brought turnips. They had fried turnips and boiled turnips, and Doris tried to think of other ways to cook turnips. But they said they never really went hungry. God always provided. Sometimes it would just be biscuits and gravy or turnips, but they gave God thanks for it all.

The ministry was not too well organized. Licenses were not required or issued. If a man felt a call to preach, he preached whenever and wherever he could find a place and someone to listen. Bible schools were nonexistent. Young preachers learned to preach by working with other ministers, studying the Word, praying, and preaching. Often there was no warning or time to prepare a sermon ahead. During service, the pastor sometimes leaned over to a young minister and whispered, "You preach tonight." No one taught them how to take notes and outline sermons. "Just open your mouth and let God fill it" was the usual exhortation.

Once when Myrlin was about two, he fell out the door of the car as his father parked on an unpaved street. A cinder punctured a blood vessel in his forehead. Urban picked him up and prayed as the blood spurted forth with each heartbeat. Instantly the bleeding stopped. Urban's father-in-law was astonished at how quickly the blood stopped.

The Vanderhoff's daughter, Gwenelda, was born on July 18, 1937. She received the Holy Ghost at age nine.

In 1943 at a district conference in Vandalia, Illinois, Urban was ordained by the Pentecostal Church, Incorporated. That fall they located a building with a five-room apartment upstairs in Moline, Illinois. It cost them 2,500 dollars with 25 dollars down and 25 dollars a month. The nation was now in the midst of World War II, and Urban worked at International Harvester. God blessed, and in November they held their first service and laid the foundation for the Moline church.

For about seven years they labored with about thirty-five to forty in attendance. Myrlin enrolled in his first year at the Pentecostal Bible Institute of Tupelo, Mississippi.

In the fall of 1945 the Pentecostal Church, Incorporated and the Pentecostal Assemblies of Jesus Christ merged to become the United Pentecostal Church. The Vanderhoffs were at the merger conference.

The church in Moline prospered, but they felt their work was over. After Urban announced his resignation, he visited one of the elderly sisters in the church. She seemed sad, so he asked, "What's the trouble?" She didn't want him to leave, so he tried to explain that another good pastor would come. She said, "No, Brother Vanderhoff, I pray the Lord will take me home before you go." Urban preached that dear old sister's funeral before he left Moline.

After he left, Brother Latta assumed the pastorate and later his son, Samuel Latta, pastored there. The beautiful building and large congregation in Moline, now pastored by Wayne Mitchell, has come a long way from its humble beginning forty years ago in a storefront building with living space above.

Urban quit his job at International Harvester, purchased a tent, and left Moline. They held meetings at Belvedere and Jacksonville, Illinois, and revivals in other Illinois towns. While in a revival at Hillview for Brother Mann, they prayed for a man in the church who was going blind. He could no longer read and he used a white cane. God instantly healed him, and that same night he read from a song book when God restored his sight.

While in Jacksonville, Urban was called to pastor for a few years in Palmyra, Illinois, a small farming town. Myrlin returned from Bible college, met and married a lovely Christian girl, Ruth Newman, and they evangelized.

The Vanderhoffs left Illinois to go to Antigo in northern Wisconsin. At this time their daughter, Gwenelda, had finished high school and left for the Pentecostal Bible Institute. While there she met and married another student, Allan Oggs, who was called to the ministry.

While at Antigo, Urban met a Church of God minister, Reverend Stiegle. Through visitation over about two years, Brother Steigle received the truth of baptism in Jesus' name. He taught it to his people and they accepted it; however, neither he nor his congregation had actually put into practice what they believed by being baptized. A February snowstorm caused icy roads during a district conference in Clintonville, Wisconsin. Brother Steigle later related that while en route to the conference, he lost control of his car and it headed for the river. When he saw where he was headed he thought, And I haven't been baptized in Jesus' name! He regained control of the car and went on to conference, where Urban baptized him and all the members of his church.

Brother Carl Thurston resigned as pastor of the church in Dowageic, Michigan, and the church contacted Urban. After seven years in Wisconsin, he accepted the Dowageic church. God blessed abundantly for twelve years in that work.

During that first year in Dowageic, he painted houses in Niles, Michigan, for Brother Gentry of the Pentecostal Assemblies of the World. One day while painting in the gable end of the house, he put a ladder upon the porch roof to reach it. From that time on, until he awoke in the hospital a week later, he had no memory of what happened. He had climbed the ladder and was putting on the first brush of paint when the ladder slipped off the roof and he landed head first on the sidewalk. Brother Gentry said, "When I turned him over, there was no breath in him. I called on the Lord and when I said, 'Jesus,' he began to breathe." When he got to the hospital, the doctors found that he had broken both wrists, one shoulder, and three ribs. One rib had punctured a lung, and he also had a brain concussion plus many cuts and bruises. He was hospitalized six weeks. He said, "Had Brother Gentry not called on the name of Jesus on my behalf, I would not be alive today." Eventually he returned to pastoring and remained there over twelve years.

Doris had been in poor health for several years, and in 1974 she passed away. Shortly afterward, Urban resigned the church, and David Helmuth became the new pastor. Brother Vanderhoff decided to evangelize, and he preached in Iowa, Wisconsin, Illinois, and Nebraska for about two years.

His travels took him into South Carolina, for revivals, and there he met a widow with two sons in the church in Conway. Her name was also Doris and she became his second wife. Since Urban had spent his life working in small churches, starting new works in towns without a Jesus Name church, home missions was his heart's desire. One day the Vanderhoffs were visiting in Dillon, South Carolina and both of them felt led to start a work for His name here. They pastored for ten years until his health began to fail. He passed away September 11, 1988.

Doris McKee Vanderhoff, Urban Vanderhoff, Myrlin and Gwenelda.

Urban T. Vanderhoff

Rev. and Mrs. Vanderhoff, family and friends.

Three generations of Vanderhoffs: Urban, Myrlin, and Arthur, 1981.

27

H. EARL WILSON

by Dianne Cothern

The earliest memories I have of my grandfather, H. Earl Wilson, are sitting on his lap and combing his white, wavy hair. He teased me and said, "If I didn't pick on you, you'd think I was mad at you!" I loved to hear the stories of his experiences while he was an evangelist and pastor and of the miracles God did for him and his family.

He was born soon after the turn of the century to a Methodist preacher and his wife. In his early childhood his father accepted the message about the Holy Ghost and later the truth of baptism in Jesus' name. While studying the first chapter of Hebrews, he received the revelation of the mighty God in Christ.

As a child, Earl felt the call of God to the ministry. He had been preaching the Jesus Name gospel for several years before he met and married the daughter of a pioneer of the gospel from Arkansas.

Brother Clifton was in a revival at Mayflower, but so far nothing had happened. Some friends of his went to the meeting and took Earl Wilson. Although Earl had never preached before, word got to Brother Clifton that his friends were bringing a minister. They had a flat tire and arrived just as the preacher began. Brother Clifton told the congregation, "We have a young preacher here tonight to bring the message. They had a flat coming out from Little Rock and he's tired. Everyone come back tomorrow night and bring someone with you to hear the new preacher."

For weeks Isaiah 1:18—"Come now, and let us reason together, saith the LORD: though your sins be as scarlet, they shall be as white as snow; though they be red like crimson, they shall be as wool"—had been running through Earl's mind. All day he fasted and prayed down by a creek that ran through the pasture where he was staying. When he got up to preach that night, he said, "I take for my text tonight Isaiah 1:18." Then the anointing of God came on him, and when he gave the altar call, fifteen fell in the altar.

From there Grandpa Earl and Brother Clifton went to Conway and took turns preaching. One night Brother Clifton was so hoarse he could only whisper, "You'll have to preach." Grandpa was hoarse himself. When he got up, he said, "As you know, this is Brother Clifton's night to preach but he can only whisper and I'm not much better. We'll have preaching if the preacher comes. I'm taking for my subject 'Bobbed Hair.' " Again God spoke through him, and people told him that he floated about a foot above the platform as he preached. When he gave the altar call, fourteen girls with bobbed hair went to the altar.

One of the girls was dating a bootlegger. Grandpa told her she could not go with him anymore now that she was a Christian. When the bootlegger came for her, she told him she could not go with him. "Why?" he asked. When she told what Grandpa had instructed her, he said, "I'll teach him not to meddle in my affair." He threatened to beat Grandpa up so badly that "his folks won't know him."

Grandpa knew that the bootlegger carried a fortyeight pistol, a steel dagger, and a pair of brass knuckles. He prayed, "Lord, if you can get more glory out of my life by my being killed or in the hospital, I want you to have the glory no matter what."

One Sunday he stayed after the others had gone. When everyone had left, the bootlegger said, "I'm going to beat you up right now. I know I can." Over six feet tall, he weighed more than two hundred pounds.

"I know you can, too, and if you had said so a few months back, I'd have told you to prove it. But now, I'm a Christian, and by the grace of God, if you knock me down, I'll get up and turn the other cheek," Grandpa answered.

The bootlegger began to weep and never touched Grandpa. When folks asked him why, he said, "I don't know, but when that little preacher said what he did, I couldn't hit him. There was something in him, around him, or something."

Irby Bailey similarly testified, "As a young man I lived about three miles from the Sunny Lane community, where I attended church. A devout family held prayer meetings in their home and a young minister, Earl Wilson, was at one prayer meeting. Something about him stood out to me. He did everything with all his might. One of his favorite songs went, 'Oh, I know I don't feel blue, for I'm rich and happy too.' Brother Wilson sang with so much enthusiasm, the rafters of the house echoed. He preached with the same zeal. Years after, my wife and I received the Holy Ghost, were baptized in Jesus' name, and accepted the call to the ministry; then I understood why Brother Wilson was so thrilled."

While attending a conference in Beaumont, Texas, with Brother Wilburn, Grandpa joined the evangelistic band of W. H. Lyon and they went to Comanche, Texas. One night Grandpa preached on the subject "Jesus and What He Can Do." After church a young couple came up carrying a baby. They showed Grandpa the baby's feet, a pitiful sight. Instead of normal feet, they turned up the back of the leg. "Can Jesus heal our baby's feet?" they asked.

"Oh, yes, He can," Grandpa said as he laid a hand on each foot and prayed. He felt the feet turn to the proper position. They were completely normal! Years later, Grandpa was in a street meeting in Comanche when a woman asked him, "Do you remember me?" She was the mother of that baby. "He's marching in the United States Army now!"

From Comanche, the band went to Muleshoe, Texas, and then to Clovis, New Mexico, establishing churches all along. From New Mexico they went to Farwell, Texas, where Brother Lyon pastored for many months, sending Grandpa on to fill an appointment in Littlefield.

While there, he preached the longest sermon of his career. He spoke in a crowded schoolhouse with standing room only. Reading Jeremiah 6:16 for a text, he spoke for two hours and forty-five minutes on "Old Paths." Again people who were there said he floated above the floor. He reminded them of the length of the sermon, but they just said, "It didn't seem like fifteen minutes."

After two years and eight months with Brother Lyon's band, Grandpa went home. He visited some friends in Little Rock, Arkansas, and G. Hobart Brown asked him to hold a revival. "We've not had a real move of God in some time and we need a good revival." The Lord did move in a mighty way. One woman who had been seeking the Holy Ghost for fourteen years was filled. Twenty-eight repented, fourteen were filled with the Holy Ghost, and the revival spirit continued long after the meeting closed. Following this meeting Grandpa was the conference evangelist.

He went back home near Star City, Arkansas, where there was much moonshine and bootlegging. During one service, Grandpa noticed people going out and coming back in. He felt the power of the devil but couldn't fathom what was wrong. The people had heard that someone had come to kill him, and they had gotten their guns to protect him.

After dismissing, Grandpa saw a man out from the brush arbor. He felt led to speak to him. Grandpa asked him, "Are you a Christian?" The man cursed and said, "No!" Grandpa told him, "You'd better be, or that's where you are going." This man was the ringleader of those who were going to kill Grandpa and also the brother of the woman in whose home he was staying. Some people with guns were waiting for a signal from him, but no harm came to Grandpa.

Grandpa held a six-week brush arbor revival at Hardin, Arkansas. He baptized eighty-nine and sixty-five were filled with the Holy Ghost. From this revival a Sunday school began and a church was built.

Edith Hayes from Hardin reminisces about those

revival days: "Brother Wilson came back for a revival in the Junett community. The Hardin church went to help. Ed Donaldson drove a truck loaded with people; others drove their cars. The Lord blessed from the first night in that old brush arbor. Not everyone could get under the arbor, so they stood outside. Before services every evening, the women went in one direction and the men in another into the woods for prayer. Many people received the Holy Ghost every night.

"One night a demon-possessed man came to the altar. He wanted to kill, so Brother Earl said, 'Everyone who is not prayed up, stand back!' Then he said, 'Down, in Jesus' name!' The man fell to his knees, as if he had been hit in the head. He came back again and Brother Earl said again, 'Down in Jesus' name!' Then he told Satan that he was bound. The next day the saints fasted and prayed all day. The man was set free, received the Holy Ghost, and lived for God until he died. Some of his children still come to church.

"Another night Brother Earl gave the altar and pleaded with souls. He gave a message saying that one in the group would not hear the dove in the spring. Sure enough, a young man died from a knife stab in just a short while."

After the Hardin engagement, Grandpa went to Friendship, Arkansas, as pastor, then to Arkadelphia as pastor, then back to Hardin as pastor. There he married. He stayed as pastor for over a year after his marriage, then left and went to Pine Bluff to pastor. There his first child, Juanita Marie, was born. Then the family went to Trumann, Arkansas, for a revival and he stayed on as pastor. He pastored there until after the birth of his second child, Merlin Dean, leaving in the late winter of 1936.

The Wilson family had some miraculous experiences there. During a revival one Sunday morning before breakfast, a man knocked at the door and asked for prayer for his wife. "She's had a stroke!" Grandpa went and prayed for her, and she was healed instantly.

After church that same Sunday, the Wilsons went home with one of the deacons for lunch. While they were eating, a boy came and said, "Daddy wants you to come and pray for Mother." Grandpa told him, "I'll come when we finish eating." A short time later, the grown son came and said, "Hurry, Mother's dying! The doctor says she won't live through the day!" When Grandpa got there, a grown daughter had fainted from grief, the son was on one side of the bed, and the husband was holding the woman's hand and crying as she was in a coma. Grandpa prayed and God healed the woman instantly.

From there they went to another woman who had suffered a stroke, and God healed her. Then from there to a woman who was bent double. God healed again. Then they prayed for a woman in her eighties who had been crippled in a car wreck and had walked on crutches for eight months. Grandpa felt led to ask her if she wanted a drink of water. The daughter brought her one. Grandpa set the glass on the floor, took her crutches, and said, "Grandma, in the name of Jesus, reach down and get that glass." She did so.

Grandpa also had another miraculous experience while pastoring in 1936. One Sunday afternoon when he was lying down, God flashed verses of Scripture—book, chapter, and verse—in front of him as though on a screen. He called for Grandma to read the verses as they came. They started with Matthew 5:20.

That Sunday night he preached on those passages and the message stirred up much anger. Guilty ones stopped his pay, trying to starve him out. But God caused a young man who was working in a bakery to bring the Wilsons cakes, pies, and bread. They depended upon their cow for the baby's milk, but the cow had no hay or feed. The last stick of firewood was gone. When Grandpa and Grandma got up from prayer, Grandma looked out the window and saw someone pulling in the driveway. She saw a bale of hay lying on top of a load of wood and cried, "Hey, hey! Well, it *is* hay!" The man bringing it was one of the angry ones. He had gone out to his farm, but when he got ready to return to town, God had him to load his pickup with wood and the bale of hay. The man drove back to Grandpa's shed and asked, "Where do you want this? God made me bring it."

The Assembly of God pastor called Grandpa to his house and loaded his car down with potatoes, fruit, and things from his cellar. "Come back if you need anything," he added. A Church of God pastor killed a cow, and God told him to take a quarter to that One God preacher. He went and knocked on Grandpa and Grandma's door. Grandpa went to the door, and the preacher said very crossly, "Can you tell me where that One God preacher lives?" Grandpa did, thinking perhaps the man wanted to harm him. They went out to the truck, whereupon the preacher told him the story, and said to pick out the quarter he wanted. Grandpa said, "I won't. If God told you to bring it, He told you which one to bring." The preacher gave him the best one.

After leaving Trumann, the Wilsons held a revival in Senath, Missouri, and stayed for about two months. From there Grandpa felt led to go to Denver, Arkansas. When he got there, the pastor told him that it was not the time for a revival. They had service in Denver that night; however, and God blessed. Then the pastor said, "I feel led to have a revival!"

Later Grandpa held revivals in Sapulpa and Tulsa, Oklahoma, then went on to Vera to start a church.

During the revival in Vera, on divine healing night, a car drove up and parked. Some people got out, but two men stayed in the car. When they had prayer for the sick, the driver got out of the car and another came to help him bring an old man in to be prayed for. As the saints prayed, Grandpa took hold of his arms and raised them, and the congregation went wild. The man had not been able to raise his arms or use them. Twenty-seven doctors had said, "No chance!" God instantly healed him, and he drove his car to service the next night. He had been a member of the Church of Christ, and four other Church of Christ families came into the truth as a result.

One of the families had a midget who was twelve years old. One day after service Charles asked Grandpa, "Brother Wilson, do you think God can heal me?" "I know he can," Grandpa said. He prayed for the underdeveloped boy and God healed him. He grew to be a 160-pound man.

After establishing and pastoring the Vera church, the Wilsons went to Dewar, Oklahoma, for a revival. The pastor had left, so they became pastors there. One summer they baptized thirty-nine, and out of that number, there are three or four preachers. God gave them around two hundred souls that summer.

Grandpa told me, "I have just given you a few highlights of my early ministry. I can tell you of blind receiving their sight, deaf hearing, lame walking, cancer dropping off, the barren bearing children, curved spines straightened, and legs lengthened. For eight months food multiplied enough for four to eat. We ate all we wanted and still had enough for the next meal. We could still go to the meal and flour can and have enough for bread."

God did not forget Brother Wilson in his later years. Twice the Lord blessed him with his car. Once after he prayed, he drove fifty miles with a broken fan. The battery ran completely down, but the car did not get hot. The second time, his car caught fire and blazed two feet up in the air. He made it to a filling station, and the fire went out like a blown-out match.

Irby Bailey spoke of Grandpa preaching at his church: "His enthusiasm and zeal was still the same. His faith for divine healing, strong message of biblical holiness, and firm convictions on repentance, baptism in Jesus' name, and the infilling of the Holy Ghost have not waned with his age."

Grandpa's last pastorate was in Oklahoma City. I received the Holy Ghost in his church when I was only eight years old.

Editor's note: Earl Wilson went to be with the Lord early in 1992.

Earl, his dad, and Laman.

Earl's parents and two brothers with Earl standing in front of his mother with Bible.

The Earl Wilson family at Mt. Crest campmeeting.

Rev. and Mrs. Earl Wilson, 1956.

28

WARREN L. WOMBLE

by Maureen Michael

Visitors to the United Pentecostal Church in Paoli, Oklahoma, scarcely notice the modest frame house located across the street. The fresh paint, the neatly tended flowerbeds, and the manicured lawn indicate that the residents of the house believe it is important to keep their home in order. Those who know the elderly couple who live there know that attention to detail about natural things is an extension of their diligent, careful, and faithful walk with God.

On a wall in the house hangs a distinctive plaque that looks formal and slightly out of place among the personal treasures and ornaments accumulated over the years. It hangs over a comfortable chair where a silver-haired man sits, and it means a great deal to him. The plaque reads: "A salute to fifty years of service in the ministry—For integrity and character—Devotion to duty—Excellent standards—Exemplary leadership—Proclamation of truth." The United Pentecostal Church International presented this plaque to Warren L. Womble in his ninety-fifth year.

Born Warren Linnie Womble on October 11, 1890, along with his twin brother, John Henry, at Lono, Arkansas, he soon became acquainted with the hardships of life. His grandparents had migrated from Tennessee to homestead in the south-central part of Arkansas in 1885. His parents, John Warren and Malinda Womble, moved to southeast Texas, where his father died an untimely death just a few months before the birth of the twin boys. He is buried in what was known as the Whiterock Cemetery near Crockett, Texas.

After his father's death, his mother returned to Arkansas, where he was born. Without a father, he would also not know the love of a mother, for the record shows his mother died on October 15, 1890, just four days after his birth, leaving four orphaned children to the mercies of the world. His own recollections of his early childhood and the following years are told in his own words:

"My brother and I, though twins, were not at all identical. He was said to be fair complexioned, and his hair had a red cast, while I was dark skinned with black hair. My oldest sister, our sometime babysitter, said I cried excessively, but my brother was very quiet. We did not have the pleasure of growing up together and sharing our blessings and troubles with each other, for in a short time we were separated. Our paternal grandparents, John Jabus and Sarah Elizabeth (Sasser) Womble, took the oldest girl and my brother. Our maternal grandparents took the youngest girl and me. Then in 1892, at the age of eighteen months, my brother passed away.

"My sister and I lived on the old homestead with our grandmother, an uncle, and two aunts. The surrounding country was very sparsely settled. Three miles south stood our post office, and about the same distance the other way sat the one-room school we attended. Only three dwellings dotted the distance between our house and the school. Often it was dark before we got home.

"Those who cared for us did the best they could. They supplied our needs as they were able. Best of all, my grandmother was a devout Christian and read her Bible. When older people visited, they sat and talked about the Scriptures. I listened wholeheartedly. She instilled what she knew about the Word of God into my very being, and it has never left me. When I sought the Lord in 1922 for a closer walk with Him, I had a vision in which my grandmother appeared very vividly. We attended the Clear Creek Methodist Church.

"After a short time, our uncle left us and went to Friendship, Arkansas. I loved Uncle Jacob Samuel Bailey and was glad when he came to visit us. The two aunts took over the responsibility of farming the old place. But by the help of a good old neighbor, Uncle Mack Phillips, who advised and did some hauling for us, we made it. After a number of years, my uncle bought a place at Friendship and moved us there in April 1901.

"Everything was different here. He took full responsibility and we were just helpers. The land was fertile here on the Ouachita River. A good farmer and a hard worker, my uncle taught me a lot about farming. I helped him do anything I was big enough to do. He told others he'd as soon have me to help on the farm as any man in Friendship. That made me feel grown up. We forded the river to the farm when it was low enough; if not we crossed on the ferry. Finally the county built a bridge. The school was much better here. We had a four-room grade school, two churches, a post office, and stores not far from us.

"I attended the Methodist church in this little village. At one time, Mrs. Deal, wife of the school principal, was my Sunday school teacher. She encouraged me to attend church regularly, saying she saw something within me that, if cultivated, would make a useful man of God. But I am sorry to say, I did not altogether take her advice, for I drifted with a rough element for a while, though never to extremes."

As a young man Brother Womble attended telegraph school and got a job as an apprentice to a telegraph operator on the Missouri Pacific Railroad. Even though he was not a Christian at this time, he soon knew that it was not best for him to spend his life around the rough element that followed the railroad. God guided him another direction. In the following years he farmed and taught school for about fifteen years.

Then God began to bring about events that radically changed his destiny. Near the little town of Friendship, Arkansas, there were two churches of the most common denominations prevalent in that day. As almost everyone in the community did, he attended one of those churches. But God had other plans.

Soon the tranquility of traditional religion in the little community was disturbed. A preacher of a "new gospel" arrived on the scene, C. P. Kilgore. Traveling in a team and wagon, his family almost perished fording a rain-swollen creek on the edge of town. The wagon was swept downstream by the rushing torrent, and for perilous moments it looked as if disaster could not be averted. But the Lord delivered the family from the churning waters, and they journeyed on into town.

The "storm" was not over for the evangelist, however, as his message did not please the denominational churches in the area. Denied the opportunity to preach in these churches, he began preaching the Apostolic message in storefronts, on porches, and finally in an open-air tabernacle constructed with whatever material was available.

During this time God began to deal with Brother Womble. He reflected on his own recollections of events leading to his conversion: "Even though I attended another church, I began to feel drawn to the tabernacle. I began to search the Scriptures to disprove the doctrine preached there. My studies only confirmed it. I began attending the services, and before long I was baptized in the name of Jesus and received the Holy Ghost on August 31, 1922. God also permitted me to see a glorious vision. I saw an angel standing with his back to me. Over his shoulder, I saw a large book with clean, white pages. As I watched, the angel took a pen and, in large bold letters, wrote my name plainly in the Book of Life. In the background, I saw my grandmothcr.

"Soon after this I definitely felt my call to the ministry. Now I understood why I had never really succeeded in any of my former undertakings."

God did not intend for Brother Womble to enter the ministry alone. On October 17, 1928, he married Lona Kizziar, who helped for many years on the field. A daughter, Maureen, and a son, John, were born during the Depression years.

Brother Womble took the lead in his home church when it had no pastor. He taught the Bible class and conducted cottage services. He was ordained to the ministry at Arkadelphia, Arkansas, in 1936 by C. E. Carter, S. L. Wise, and C. A. Pyatt.

Brother Womble pastored churches throughout Arkansas and Oklahoma. During the early years there was little income from pastoring the small country churches, so he worked at farm labor. On one occasion he worked for the Work Projects Administration to meet the needs of his family. Despite the meager income the Lord wonderfully provided, and there was always food on the table. Often one member of the church brought a pig, another corn, and along with the garden produce and eggs, the family always managed. Money, however, remained scarce.

Pioneer ministers learned to trust God completely for even bare necessities of life. Every church was a "home mission" church. Many memories of people and places, joys and sorrows, and an era perhaps never to be repeated, still linger today. All-day services on Mother's Day, with dinner under the shade of giant oak trees, were special times when life did not move at the hectic pace it does today.

One of the special joys for Brother and Sister Womble has always been the cards, letters, and occasional visits from the second and third generation of former saints that they have pastored. Many of them are in the ministry and work of the Lord today.

One significant fact in Brother Womble's ministry is that he pastored every church at least twice, with the exception of the church he was pastoring when he retired. He left each church with a good report and was welcomed back if the Lord led in that direction. He is pleased that, of all the couples he has married over the years, he does not know of a single divorce.

Brother Womble served as presbyter of Oklahoma District Section 5 in 1955. Over the years he has been a prolific writer. A frequent contributor of articles to the *Beacon,* he has also written a book on the plan of salvation. His ministry through the written word has touched many.

Brother Womble retired from pastoral work in 1957. Since that time he and Sister Womble have resided in Paoli, where they have remained faithful to their home church. He has this to say about those years: "My wife and I, who have shared the blessings and troubles of life together for the past years, are just waiting and serving the best we can, looking for 'that blessed hope, and the glorious appearing of the great God and Saviour Jesus Christ' (Titus 2:13) to convey us to that perfect place, our eternal abode. 'We are journeying unto the place of which the LORD said, I will give it you: come thou with us' (Numbers 10:29)."

Rev. and Mrs. Warren L. Womble, Friendship, Arkansas, church and parsonage, 1938.

Bro. and Sis. Womble, John and Maureen, Bismark Arkansas, church, 1942.

Bro. and Sis. Womble, Paoli, Oklahoma, church.

Bro. Womble in revival at St. Charles, Arkansas. 1941.